W9-BHV-281

FULL CIRCLE

RESTORING YOUR HABITAT
TO WILDERNESS

*To Jan —
Remember all the
great times we had?
Please come visit.*

Bayliss "Rock" Prater

BAYLISS PRATER & KATHLEEN McNEAL

This book is based upon a decade of HOW TO programs at the Last Resort Wilderness Area, in an effort to restore wildlife so that humans and animals can live in harmony. The Last Resort received the 1991 Ohio Governor's Conservation Achievement Award and the 1992 National Wildlife Federation's Soil Conservationist Award, presented by the League of Ohio Sportsmen. Also, in 1992, The Ohio Alliance for the Environment presented the Last Resort with a Certificate of Recognition for distinguished service in the field of environmental education.

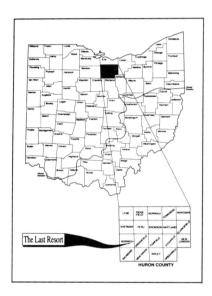

Copyright © 1993 by Last Resort Press

Published by
Last Resort Press
2359 Miller Road
Willard, OH 44890

All rights reserved including the right of
reproduction in whole or in part in any form.

Printed in New Washington, Ohio, U.S.A. by Herald Printing Co., Inc.

Printed with soya ink on recycled paper

ISBN 0-9635867-1-8

ACKNOWLEDGEMENTS

A very special debt of gratitude goes to Rock's parents, Russell and Millie Prater, for their more than 20 year stewardship of the acres that have become the Last Resort Wilderness Area. Their efforts gave us a jump start.

Much of the information was obtained from the Ohio Department of Natural Resources (ODNR) and the U.S. Fish and Wildlife Service (FWS). A special thank you to John Daugherty and Luther Miller of ODNR Division of Wildlife and to Charles Blair of the U.S. Fish and Wildlife Service for their expertise and assistance.

Many of our friends and relatives read, edited and encouraged us including Janet and Joe Androsac, Anthony Cavello, Terry Lutz, Jimmy Montgomery, Bob Secor, Holly Fackler and Jim Norrocky. Thanks to our niece China Williams and Jeff and Nadean Traylor of Backroad Chronicles for their editing, encouragement and expertise.

Our gratitude goes to Art Weber for his permission to use the front cover photo. Kathleen took the picture of Rock trapping muskrats and the FWS provided the photos of the ducks and pheasant. All other photos were taken by Rock. Molly Stewart drew Figure 1 - Map of the Last Resort Wilderness Area.

Lastly, our appreciation to all the wild things that have rewarded our efforts through the acceptance of us as equal in our quest for coexistence.

DEDICATION

In the forward of **A Sand County Almanac,** Aldo Leopold states: "There are some who can live without wild things, and some who cannot."

This book is dedicated to the efforts of all of YOU who cannot live without wild things and are going about the business of doing something about it.

CONTENTS

PREFACE

We are usually asked two questions: why are we restoring farmland to wildlife habitat and how is it accomplished? We have many reasons. You, the reader, must have a few reasons or you wouldn't have picked up this book. FULL CIRCLE answers the "how to" rather than the "why" but the introduction is our way to spread the message.

Wildlife is dying for habitat. Since we, as humans, need wildlife and wild places and since modern ways have destroyed natural habitat and reduced wildlife populations, habitat restoration is a necessity. Habitat restoration is not necessarily a pleasant pastime. Often it's hard work. We've planted trees and shrubs in early spring when the weather was winter. Our arms and shoulders ached so we could hardly lift them. Our hands were raw and muddy and beyond feeling. What kept us going was the vision of the trees and shrubs growing, only to have that dashed later on by a severe drought. Sometimes we want to give up, live in a condo. **Habitat restoration requires dedication.** Dedication to working beyond sore muscles, beyond arguing with the township mower; most of all dedication to time. For trees to grow and vegetation to cover worn out soil takes time. The payoff is not in money but in being part of nature restoring itself.

Our area of Ohio was once covered by a series of glaciers. These glaciers left many scoured out areas that became wetlands. Prairie grasses and then trees moved in. The climate following the glacier era was probably cooler than ours now. What does all this have to do with restoring habitat? We increase our chances of success if we take into consideration what occurred here naturally along with the present climatic conditions. The glaciers made farming possible by depositing rich till. The soil was made rich by aeons of decomposing grasses, wetland plants, and later leaves from deciduous trees. To make way for farming, the trees were cut down. Today, remnants of the great forests remain in fragmented places, mostly those too wet for farming. More than 99% of Ohio's landscape has been altered.

To restore our small part of Ohio, we realized that we needed to restore the wetlands. Since wildlife requires water, food, shelter, breeding and nesting spots, wetlands have been a major part of our restoration program. Other components or strands of the program are bird feeders, food plots and food producing shrubs; nesting or roosting boxes and places for perching; grasses and legumes for shelter, nesting, and food. We follow the rule of diversity: the more diverse the habitat, the more diverse the wildlife. Our diversity includes grassland, old field, old orchard and old pasture, yard area, woodland, riparian (creek and bottom land hardwood wetland), wetlands and scrubby areas.

THIS BOOK SHOULD PROVIDE SOMETHING FOR EVERYONE. Not all people will be able to set aside for wildlife more than a small space but each of us can contribute something.

In spite of the hard work and temporary setbacks, there are many rewards. We have the reward of knowing that we are part of regenerating the land, that we are restoring at least a part of the web of life. That is a long term reward and rather abstract. Sometimes we need something now.

Frequently that is when nature rewards us in simple but elegant ways. Maybe it's the Northern Oriole who flies back and forth in front of our large window so we notice he has returned for the summer. Sometimes, while explaining to a doubting visitor that indeed the wildlife does seem to acknowledge and appreciate what we are providing, something extraordinary happens. One or two bluebirds will fly in front of us, catching the sun in a mind dazzling display of brilliant blue. It's having our hunting neighbors tell us that the big buck they have been tracking for several years gives up his regular circuit during hunting season and stays close to this place.

If you, like many of our friends, doubt that wildlife appreciates and acknowledges your effort, **leave a place for wildlife and see what happens.**

We are writing a companion source and plan book to FULL CIRCLE that will include plans for bird boxes, feeders, lists of suppliers and other references. If you'd like more information or have information to share, we'd like to hear from you.

Kathleen McNeal & Bayliss (Rock) Prater
Managers
Last Resort Wilderness Area
2359 Miller Road
Willard, OH 44890

INTRODUCTION

"Why are you restoring your 78 acre farm into a game preserve and bird sanctuary?" is one of the more frequent questions put to us. The choice to create a wilderness area from this piece of rural paradise wasn't an easy one. The Last Resort is located in a glaciated county where 80 percent of the land is farmed; 93 percent of that is classified as "prime agricultural land". Mostly row crops are grown here—corn, soybeans, some small grains, with some specialty crops of vegetables, fruits, tomatoes and sugar beets. That's not the way it used to be.

Before the 1950s, the typical midwestern farm had small fenced fields. These fields consisted of corn, hay, pasture for a small dairy herd, small grains, a woodlot and an orchard. This means of farming provided for the farm family. It also provided food and habitat for many species of wildlife.

These same family farms have undergone extensive change. The small fields have been united with adjoining fields to create massive fields of soybeans and corn. Fence and tree lines have been bulldozed or allowed to fall into decay. Wetlands have been drained. Streams have been straightened and land cleared. Urban and suburban acreage has increased, as has industrialization in rural areas.

The bottom line for native species has been a huge loss in the wildlife habitat base. In one 3,000-year period of the Pleistocene during which great numbers of organisms perished, North America lost about 50 mammalian species and 40 birds species or about three species per hundred years. Since the arrival of the Puritans at Plymouth Rock in 1620, over 500 species and subspecies of native animals and plants have become extinct. At this rate, worldwide, it is estimated that 15 to 25 percent of all known species may become extinct by the turn of the century. Locally, some once abundant populations such as woodcock, bobwhite quail, grouse, bob-o-link, and dickcissel are now rare.

Returning acreage to wildlife habitat became a quest for us. With the help of the Ohio Department of Natural Resources (ODNR), the following factors were identified as most severely limiting the ability of native wildlife populations to survive:

*The loss of undisturbed grasses and/or legumes. In the past 25 years alone, more than 2 million acres of Ohio meadowfield have been put to other land uses.

*The loss of winter food supply. Waste grain left after harvest once supplied ample winter food. Today's new harvesters remove more of the grain and potential winter cover frequently falls to the plow before snowfall.

*The removal of woody and shrubby cover found in small woodlots, fencerows, backyards, and other odd areas. Putting marginal land into agricultural production, urbanization, and the expansion of suburbs have expedited the loss of this key component of upland wildlife habitat. Thus, upland species have no protected areas of access to crop fields for feeding.

The 52 acres of the Last Resort which were tilled have been placed in the U.S. Department of Agriculture's Conservation Reserve Program (CRP), drawing a modest annual income. Hundreds of pounds of timothy, red clover, ladino clover, alsike clover, bird's foot trefoil, orchard grass, bromegrass, switchgrass, and many others, all approved by ODNR, have been planted. Now many types of grasses and legumes on the Last Resort provide much needed cover.

About five acres of wildlife food plots are planted annually. The plots consist of black oil sunflowers, buckwheat, white Proso millet and dwarf grain sorghum. Each location is carefully selected to allow protection for the wildlife.

More than 5,000 shrubs, including 17 different varieties of native Ohio shrubs, have been planted along with hundreds of trees. Seventeen more varieties are on the long-range plan for planting. Areas that were cleared in the farming frenzy of the 1970s are being replaced with shrubby habitat. Each type of shrub provides habitat and food for specific animals, especially for birds.

Life cannot exist without water. The replacement of drained wetlands has been a major priority. With the help of government agencies such as the U.S. Department of Agriculture, Ohio Department of Natural Resources, and the Department of Interior's Fish and Wildlife Service, more than 15 acres of wetlands exist on the Last Resort. Since the development of the wetlands 14 additional species have been added to our bird list.

Along with loss of habitat, erosion occurs because of modern farming techniques. The rain that falls on Ohio originally fell on forested land where the canopy tempered the downpour. It has been said that at the beginning of the 1600s a squirrel could travel from Lake Erie to the Ohio River without leaving the trees. What runoff that did occur was captured by wetlands. Today the rain falls on bare fields along gentle slopes. The runoff carries rich topsoil, along with residues of pesticides and fertilizers, into ditches designed to carry the water away.

A recent "Sustainable Agriculture" newsletter published by the Ohio State University Sustainable Agricultural Program, stated that 70 million tons of Ohio soil are washed from fields each year. This translates to 1,166,666 freight cars carrying 60 tons each. Such a train would be 9,943 miles long. If you were to watch this train go by a station at 10 mph for 24 hours every day, it would take 41 days to see the entire train pass. It costs Ohio more than $160 million per year to clean up the ditches, streams and rivers clogged by erosion.

Before CRP, our 52 tilled acres lost around 7 tons per acre per year. Each year since CRP, we take pleasure in knowing that 364 tons of topsoil remain on the land, staying put, instead of entering the waterways. Over the ten years of the CRP agreement, 3,640 tons of topsoil will be saved. That's a 60-car train! We'd be tempted to gloat if soil erosion weren't such a deadly serious problem. Soil sustains us and is part of our natural heritage. It belongs to all or to none. If we're not careful, there will be none - no topsoil, no habitat, no life.

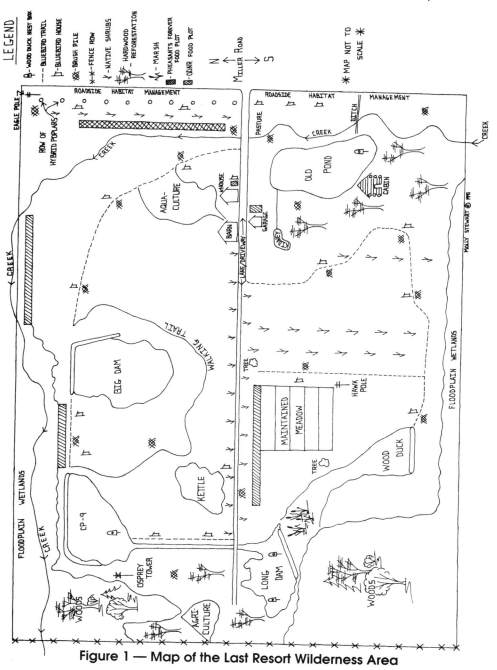

Figure 1 — Map of the Last Resort Wilderness Area

WETLANDS

Wetlands are "in" at all levels of government. Numerous studies chronicle their loss. A recent report to Congress by the Department of Interior's U.S. Fish and Wildlife Service estimates that **more than one half of the wetland acres have been lost since colonial times in the lower 48 states.**

Based on historical agricultural and soil records, the U.S. Fish and Wildlife Service publication "Wetland Status and Trends in the Conterminous United States Mid-1780s to Mid-1980s" outlines wetland losses during the past two centuries and compares current wetland acreage to that of the 1780s. According to the report, 22 of the 50 states have lost at least half of their wetlands, mostly because of conversion to agriculture. **Highlights of the report follow:**

* More than 60 acres of wetlands have been lost every hour for the past 200 years in the contiguous U.S.
* Ten states have lost more than 70% of their original wetlands: Arkansas, California, Connecticut, Illinois, Iowa, Kentucky, Maryland, Missouri and Ohio.
* California has lost the highest percentage (91%), while Alaska has lost the lowest (a fraction of one percent).

* Except for Alaska, Hawaii, and New Hampshire, no state has lost less than 20 percent of its historical wetlands.

* Florida has the second largest loss—nearly 9.3 million acres—but still has 11.0 million acres, Louisiana is second in total wetlands with 8.7 million acres left. Florida is 30% wetlands while Louisiana is 28% wetlands.

* Roughly one third of the nation's total wetland loss has taken place in the midwestern farm states of Ohio (90%), Indiana (87%), Illinois (85%), Iowa (82%), Michigan (50%), Wisconsin (46%) and Minnesota (42%).

Leading this group of seven midwestern states responsible for the third greatest loss of the nation's wetlands is Ohio, where only 10% of all original wetlands remain. Ohio is second only to California in wetland loss. Of Ohio's 5,000,000 acres of historical wetlands, about 500,000 acres remained through the 1980s. The acres destroyed within a 200 year period represents a 90% loss and only one percent less than California.

More than 20,000 acres of wetlands are lost each year in the Lower Great Lakes and St. Lawrence Basin. Less than 10% of the wetlands originally found along the shores of Lake Erie exist today. Ownership is divided among the federal and state governments, private clubs, and individuals.

Value of Wetlands

What is the value of wetlands? Half of the nation's endangered species require wetland habitats to complete their life cycles. More specifically, of Ohio's 36 endangered birds, mammals, reptiles, and amphibians, 14 rely on wetlands for at least part of their life cycle. In addition, one third of the state's rare plants are wetland species. Wetland loss is the second leading cause of wildlife endangerment in Ohio.

If saving these species of plants and animals were not enough, in agricultural areas such as ours, herbicides and inorganic and organic fertilizers are carried by the soil into streams and eventually into the remaining wetlands of Lake Erie. In Huron County the average annual soil loss is 13 tons per acre.

Wetlands can make the water cleaner because they filter sediments and absorb nutrients and other wastes and chemicals. **Wetlands could be the most effective way to deal with nonpoint source pollution such as agricultural, residential and roadway runoff.**

Wetlands can also be used to reduce or eliminate source pollution from septic tanks. The Last Resort Aquaculture wetland was designed and installed in November 1990, in part to scrub the domestic sewage outfall. The outfall now provides nutrients to the plant aquaculture area. The use of constructed wetlands and associated aquatic plant systems for municipal wastewater treatment is well documented. Most wetland treatment systems have been for municipal purposes. To our knowledge, our wetland is the first designed to treat private sewage. We know that some country homeowners simply run their outfalls to a pond or creek with no tertiary treatment. Wetlands make sense.

During dry periods, many wetlands provide drought relief by connecting surface and ground water sources, allowing ground water to increase stream flow. During wet periods, wetlands are equally valuable, acting as a sponge to absorb and store water. During heavy rains, wetlands hold the water. The water is then released gradually. The gradual release eases flood damage. The millions of dollars in flood damages suffered each year by Ohio communities could be reduced or prevented by re-establishing wetlands in floodplains.

Although "spared" by development, many wetlands are so severely affected by nearby development and farming around them that they lose their ability to function. The loss of wetlands is already being felt by Ohioans. For instance, homeowners along Ohio's north shore have been losing their homes to record high Lake Erie water levels. These were homes built on lands that until recently had been undisturbed wetlands.

From a wildlife standpoint, wetlands are our most productive habitat, with an endless variety of animal and plant life. In Ohio, 17 mammals, 56 birds, 23 reptiles and 20 amphibians utilize wetland habitats for breeding. We added 14 additional species of birds to our list within the first year of wetland restoration. Migratory birds hop from wetland to wetland seeking critical resting, nesting and feeding areas. According to recent research, the reproductive potential of migrant birds is influenced by the availability and quality of these stopover wetlands. The birds arrive at their breeding grounds in healthier condition when they are able to find sufficient food and resting areas during migration.

The shrinking numbers of waterfowl and other wildlife can be traced to America's destruction of wetlands. In 1986, wildlife biologists saw the smallest migration of ducks on record. The 66 million count was far below the annual average of 100 million in the 1970's. Waterfowl are the most prominent and economically important group of migratory birds in North America. Waterfowl are big business, generating a direct contribution to the economy in excess of several billion dollars annually.

The U.S. and Canada signed the North American Waterfowl Management Plan (NAWMP) in 1986. As a result of this agreement, U.S. Fish and Wildlife Service had money available to restore wetlands on private lands. Since we are close to Lake Erie and since we knew more water would attract more and different types of wildlife, we have cooperated with Fish and Wildlife since 1989. Twenty percent or more of the Last Resort is now restored wetlands.

The intrinsic and aesthetic value of wetlands cannot be overstated. The sounds of the spring peepers and the sight of the American Bittern are enough to support the restoration effort. We use to have to drive to the end of the road to hear the anxiously awaited first sounds of spring, the peepers. Now, after the hush of winter is over, we are surrounded by the sometimes raucous sounds of the peepers and other amphibians.

The restoration of eight different wetlands and the resulting 15-plus acres of water has offered us the opportunity to illustrate the various methods of wetland restoration, so desperately needed to stem the wetland crisis. Since so many wetlands have been lost, restoration is a necessity. Anyone interested in habitat improvement must consider a wetland.

What is a Wetland Habitat?

Most wetlands can be identified by looking for the presence of three basic characteristics of wetlands. It must be wet, with a certain kind of soil and have certain plants present.

We say that if you sit in it and you get wet it is a wetland. **Water levels** average one to one and a half feet deep but may range from moist, saturated soil conditions to water depths greater than three feet. Wetlands receive their water from groundwater discharge (spring seepage), surface runoff and direct precipitation. Naturally, water conditions shape the character of any wetland.

The **types of soil** that make up the substrates define a wetland. Wetland soils, in their undrained state, are usually saturated, flooded or covered with water long enough during the growing season to develop conditions that favor the development of wetland vegetation. Wetland soils are often very dark and fertile.

The **types of vegetation** found growing in wetlands are used to define them. Plants such as cattails, sedges and bullrushes are commonly associated with wetlands. They prefer moist conditions to ponded water. However, there are hundreds of types of water-loving plants.

With the exception of Lake Erie's and other coastal wetlands, Ohio's wetlands are relatively small, ranging in size from one to 25 acres. Across the U.S., freshwater wetlands range from small potholes a few acres in size to large expanses of several square miles.

Wetland Types

Wetland types are divided and classified according to water depth and plant composition. Several common types of wetlands are found in Ohio.

A shallow water marsh has a water depth between six inches and three feet for an extended period of time during the growing season. These wetlands have some open water interspersed with vegetation such as cattail, bullrush, arrowhead, water plantain and bur reed.

Deep water marshes (not ponds or lakes) have an estimated water depth greater than three feet for an extended time during the growing season. Deep water marshes are primarily open water, sparsely vegetated with floating and submergent plants such as lotus, water lily and pond weed.

Wet meadows have less than six inches of water depth for an extended period during the growing season and the vegetation consists mostly of grasses and sedges. Forbs such as swamp milkweed, blue vervain, Joe-pye-weed, jewelweed and boneset can also be found. Annuals such as barnyard grass, smartweed, beggarstick and ragweed pioneer disturbed and mud flat areas.

Wet woods are dominated by trees over 15 feet and contain green ash, pin oak, swamp white oak, hackberry, and red and silver maple. Soils are usually saturated or ponded with less than three inches of water.

Scrub/shrub wetlands are dominated by shrubs such as gray, silky and red-osier dogwood, common alder, buttonbush, willow, elderberry and hardwoods less than 15 feet tall.

A **wetland complex** is composed of two or more of the above mentioned wetland types. This is a preferred wetland situation for wildlife. The Last Resort's wetlands are a complex.

Man-made changes to wetlands can cause severe changes in the wetland's make up. Wetlands are also subject to change in plant composition and structure as water depths fluctuate, caused by natural changes such as droughts. Artificial and natural changes can be beneficial, but most changes disrupt the complex water cycles, impairing the ability of a wetland to attract and sustain wildlife populations. Existing wetlands must be protected. Modified and damaged wetlands must be restored.

Management

What attracts wildlife species to a wetland? Three factors determine the attractiveness and subsequent use of wetlands: water level fluctuation, the composition and structure (height, arrangement and density) of wetland plants, and the interspersion of cover and open water. Wildlife will select the vegetative zone delineated by the water depth that best provides for their biological needs such as food and nesting.

Hemimarshes, for example, are the ideal type of wetland for wildlife. Hemimarshes have 50% open water and 50% vegetation. The following simple equation results in a quality wetland for wildlife: diversity in shallow water depths + duration of flooding + size of wetland = a diversity of vegetation zones = a diversity and abundance of wildlife.

Choosing a site for wetland restoration projects or for wetland development must be done carefully. The following must be considered: topography (gradient or contour), hydrology, soils, permits, drainage district's regulated drainage projects, dam safety requirements, and plant and animal management.

Certain physical characteristics of land identify it as being suited to wetland restoration or creation. It is worth noting that true wetlands cannot be created, only restored! The best areas for developing wetlands are drained places where former wetlands have been converted to agriculture. You want to make sure you get a wetland, attractive to plants and animals. Otherwise you will have just a wet spot.

The topography of a site can be gently rolling or relatively flat. The site should have irregular and uneven contours that create subtle breaks in elevations. Shallow wetlands cannot be developed on sites with sharp relief, steep slopes or deep ravines. Cropfields that have low depressional basins positioned to intercept surface water and poor or narrow outlets make good wetlands. It is important to select a site that will promote natural changes in water levels. A site that inherently has good topography characteristics will reduce the amount of excavation and lower the overall cost.

The hydrology (water conditions) is another important feature to consider. The following questions about the hydrology of any given site should be asked: What are the sources of water and where do they originate? What direction is the water flowing? Are there any natural outlets? Has the drainage of the area been altered from subsurface drainage tile? Can you change it? If the drainage is changed, what effect will it have on the surrounding land? Is there a high water table? How long does the water naturally stand on the site? Generally, areas where water is present for extended periods during the growing season are good sites for wetland development.

Soils should have low clay and silty clay with the capacity to store and sustain desired water levels. Hydric soils are best and have a tendency to allow for the more rapid establishment of wetland vegetation. Soil types can be identified on your property by referring to the county soil map or by contacting the Soil Conservation Service (SCS).

Size of the watershed (the number of acres of land a drainage basin is serving) and drainage patterns determine the size of the embankment (dams) and outlet structure required to impound water safely. Watershed size has a bearing on the cost of constructing (restoring) the wetland. The size of a watershed can be calculated by using a U.S. Department of Interior Geological Survey map.

Picture what the wetland site will look like when finished. Contact a wildlife biologist or a representative from the SCS to help you select a potential wetland restoration site. He or she can answer questions concerning permits and other possible restrictions.

Getting expert advice is important. The lay of the land can be deceiving even to experts. For that reason, experts rely upon sophisticated equipment to determine where the dam should be.

Wetland Design and Construction

Prior planning and proper construction are necessary to get an attractive wetland for wildlife. The primary objective of wetland creation is to emulate features of natural wetlands, especially their shallow water aspects. The site must be surveyed to determine a water line (pool size) and dam location and size, if one is required. The field data from the survey can be used for an engineering plan for the wetland and will be used by the "earth-moving" contractor as a blueprint. Your Department of Natural Resources and the Soil Conservation Service can help you survey the site and design a plan.

The three basic methods for impounding water are embankment (dike, dam or levee), dugout, and tile cut. The site determines which method will be used.

An embankment is mounded and compacted soil that stops and holds water. Use this method when the topography has either a wide, shallow draw or a low depressional area with a narrow water outlet formed between two rises or knolls in the land. A dam is placed between the two rises which intercepts and impounds (stops and holds) the water on the upstream side. The dam should have 4:1 slopes and should be under four feet high to maintain shallow water conditions.

Construct emergency spillways to serve as principle outlets during high water. If the emergency spillway fails, the dam could be severely eroded or breached. We recommend natural spillways instead of overflow pipes. Pipes, if they work at all, do not handle the excess water as efficiently as "natural" spillways during flooding conditions. Pipes also need to be checked regularly and cleaned out if necessary. Don't let anyone talk you into a pipe overflow.

Use the tile cut method in areas that are natural depressions. Cut or remove the subsurface tile that drains the area to be impounded. The wetlands formed from tile cuts are very inexpensive. Since there is no dam, there is no maintenance of the dam. Tile cuts, however, do not produce the diversity in vegetative zones that the other methods do.

Use a dugout in flat areas. This is the most expensive method employed to create shallow water wetlands. A dugout involves creating the entire pool area by means of excavation only. One advantage of this method is that the optimum water levels can be created to facilitate the development of vegetative zones that are most ideal for the desired wildlife. All you have to do is decide what wildlife you want to or can expect to attract. Check to see what depth the wildlife prefers and/or what depth the plant it feeds on prefers. Then, plan your dugout accordingly. When excavating a dugout, remove and stockpile the top strata so that it can be put in the bottom of the wetland. The seed bank for wetland vegetation is found in the top strata.

Wetland Design Specifications

There are some features that can be incorporated into almost any wetland design.

* If possible, create a variety of water depths. Wetlands should have 30% at $1/2$ to $1 1/2$ feet deep, 30% at $1 1/2$ to 3 feet deep, 20% at 3 to 4 feet deep and 20% exposed mud flats. Work with the topography and stay away from designs that confine the deep water to the middle and the shallow water to the perimeter of the wetland. You must work with the topography.

* The edges or shoreline of the wetland should be as irregular as possible with bays, peninsulas, and inlets.

* The side slopes should be soft and gentle and range from 10:1 to 16:1.
* Create elevated nesting areas around the wetland or build submerged islands from excess pool area soil. Islands raised above the water level in the pool area should only be constructed if the wetland is greater than five acres. Submerged and raised islands should be a minimum of 20 feet in diameter with gentle side slopes that are 8:1 to 10:1. Raised islands must have a settled height of no less than two feet above water level and should be planted to a nesting grass **(GRASSES AND LEGUMES)**.

Management of Adjacent Non-wetland Areas

The area surrounding a restored wetland can be managed in a way to increase the attractiveness of the wetland to wildlife and provide for the needs of non-wetland wildlife species. A grass buffer at least 50 feet wide should be established around the entire wetland. The grass buffer protects the wetland from silt and chemical runoff. The buffer also provides nesting cover for both upland and wetland wildlife.

Food plots can be planted to furnish a fall and winter food source for wildlife. Low growing shrubs can be planted on the windward side of the wetland to reduce wave action on the wetland. Brisk spring winds often make the water too rough for waterfowl, especially if the wetland is located in open and flat country **(SHRUB AND TREE)**. Nest structures can be erected for wood ducks, mallards and Canada geese **(POLES AND HOLES)**.

Dike (Dam) Maintenance

The dike or dam on an artificial wetland involves a large investment and it is wise to take proper care in maintaining them. After construction, the area should be seeded to a grass and legume cover. Brome grass, timothy or orchard grass mixed with a legume should be used to hold the soil in place and provide some nesting cover for upland nesting wildlife. Mow only to control weeds and brush and only during August to prevent nest destruction. Avoid allowing trees or brush to become established on the dike since these tend to make maintenance more difficult.

Muskrats are our biggest wetland problem at the Last Resort. They have to be controlled. The damage that burrowing muskrats can do to a dam in a short period of time is more than considerable. Muskrats can breach a dam. Without control, there would be no dam and no wetlands.

The muskrat is the largest microtine rodent in the United States. Muskrats are found in almost every aquatic habitat in Ohio. They are adapted to living underwater with their waterproof undercoat, webbed feet and laterally flattened tail. They can stay submerged for as long as 20 minutes. They are nocturnal and spend their time feeding on stems, roots, bulbs and foliage of aquatic plants. They sometimes eat animal matter such as mussels, crustaceans, snails, insects and fish.

They have several litters a year averaging 6 to 8 young per litter. A little math shows how two muskrats can be a growing problem. A muskrat may live up to four years. In spite of the damage that they do, the muskrat is the nation's most important fur bearer and its harvest is six or seven times that of any other species of fur animal, but the market is rotten!

Muskrats are rodents and rodents do very well in an environment that has been altered by human activity. Eradication is not desired nor possible. It is a matter of controlling them. If you are located near moving water, such as a stream or river, control will be more difficult. As you get rid of some, others, as if they've been waiting for a vacancy, move in.

Really only two methods to control muskrats exist. Trapping and periodic drawdowns can be used to keep muskrat populations in balance with cattail control and dike damage. Management of cattails ideally should involve a management program for muskrats. Muskrats use cattails for food and to build houses. A high density of muskrats will stop the spread of cattails and will help maintain the 1:1 ratio of open water to emergent plant cover that is desirable for ducks. Even though muskrats are a real threat to a dike, they are useful in controlling cattails. If the wetlands are being chocked by cattails, let the muskrats go until the cattails are under control.

Sometimes it is necessary to use the other method, trapping. Muskrats are not suspicious and are easily trapped. Trapping must be done during legal muskrat trapping season unless you get special permission to trap out of season. In Ohio, three types of traps are legal for trapping muskrat. These are the 110 conibear, #1 or $1\frac{1}{2}$ foothold traps and the cage, box, colony or stovepipe trap.

Traps should be set where there is evidence of an active run, burrow or feeding site. We do not use or recommend foothold traps since a muskrat will pull out of a set. Traps must be set in a way that the muskrat drowns within a few minutes of being trapped. The trap must be staked in water at least a foot deep or by placing a second stake, called a drowning stick, about 10" from the trap plate so the muskrat will become entangled and drown.

If you trap during trapping season, you can sell the pelts. Pelt prices vary from year to year. Muskrat is also edible. All trapping laws should be followed and all traps should be checked daily. Make sure you know what you're doing. When you check your traps, you want to make sure that you have a muskrat and not some other animal. If you don't want to trap or don't know how, contact a local trapper.

GRASSES AND LEGUMES

What is a Grassland Habitat?

Hundreds of pounds of grasses and legumes have been planted on the Last Resort. Grassland habitat establishment and management is a must for landowners interested in attracting upland animals such as the ring-neck pheasant, bob-o-link, dickcissel and other grassland species. As a bonus, grasses and/or legumes play a vital role in building top soil.

This section refers to land on which grasses and/or legumes constitute the dominant vegetation. The differences between grasslands and old field habitats is important in managing land for wildlife. Certain species such as pheasants and bob-o-links like a "pure" stand of grassland for nesting cover while the bobwhite quail and cottontail rabbit prefer the nesting habitat of the old fields.

In Ohio, there are two major groups of grasses; cool-season and warm-season. The cool-season grasses such as timothy, orchardgrass and bromegrass begin growth in the early spring when the conditions are cool and wet. They reach maturity by early summer if not mowed, pastured or harvested. During the hot summer months, these grasses turn brown and set seed. Then in the fall, when the weather is cool and damp, they return with increasing vitality.

Warm-season grasses such as switchgrass, big and little bluestem, and Indiangrass start growth much later in the spring and reach full maturity in late summer or early fall. These warm weather grasses provide cover during the hot summer months when the cool-season grasses are dormant.

When Native Americans lived in the area, the tall grass prairie regions were composed of warm-season grasses such as the four already mentioned. These native grasses supplied habitat and food to indigenous animals such as the prairie chicken and bison. As Ohio's prairie disappeared under the plow, these animals also disappeared.

Cool-season and warm-season grasses have advantages and disadvantages. The cool-season grasses such as timothy, bromegrass and orchardgrass are easier to plant than the warm-season grasses. Cool-season grasses, however, need to be mowed more often if the invasion of unwanted plants is a concern. Over a period of time, cool-season grass fields have to be replanted to maintain a health grassland nesting habitat for wildlife.

Most warm-season grasses provide high quality nesting cover without mowing. With proper management, a warm-season grass stand is self-sustaining. We have not established large quantities of warm-season grassland stands on the Last Resort because of the high cost and difficulty in establishment.

Value of Grassland Habitats

Even though the grasslands' greatest value is nesting cover, they do provide food in the form of seed and green plant parts. Prey such as rodents and insects are attracted by this vegetation. These prey provide food for fox, coyote, kestrel, harrier, and other hawk and owl predators. It's a pleasure to watch a harrier fly our trails in search of food during the winter months. Our barn owl restoration program relies on the grassland habitat to produce the meadow vole, a rodent which comprises most of the barn owl's diet. Even though the voles are in plentiful supply, no barn owls have nested in our nest boxes. Someday soon!

Ohio is well known for the common ring-neck pheasant, a species associated with grassland habitat. They are strictly a grassland nesting species and will not nest in woodland or dense brush land. Other wildlife species that depend on grassland habitat include the grasshopper sparrow, meadowlark, Henslow sparrow, Savannah sparrow, and bob-o-link. All of these species are found at the Last Resort.

Thirty-two percent of Ohio's total wildlife species use the grassland habitat. Most farms in our area are no longer home to many of these species caused by the increased conversion of grassland to cropland. The remaining grassy areas are extensively mowed and don't support much wildlife. The existing grassland habitat must be preserved. New habitat must be created to stem the decline of grassland-dependent wildlife populations.

Designing and Implementing a Grassland Habitat Management Plan

The first step in planning a grassland habitat is selecting a suitable site on your property. A suitable site is a field that is well drained, fertile, free from trees, and has the size required for the species that you want to attract. Grassland nesting species prefer large fields surrounded by an open edge. Pheasants need at least 10-15 acres while bob-o-links need at least 20-25 acres. These fields have the same characteristics as good farmland. However, properly managed fields smaller than 10 acres, field borders, grass waterways, grass field dividers, and wetland buffer strips have the potential to produce grassland habitat.

After the site has been selected, contact your Cooperative Extension Service or Soil Conservation Service (SCS) for a soil test. DO NOT GUESS—SOIL TEST! A soil test should be conducted in order to determine the lime and fertilizer requirements.

Fertilizer - A Word or Two

Whenever possible, we recommend the use of organic fertilizer such as compost or manure. The reconstruction or rehabilitation of the soil is an important issue, particularly with soil worn out or rendered desert-like by abusive farming. Recycling enough by-products of life to the land as compost is all that is needed to bring the soil back to life and productivity. The natural resistance against pests and disease should also return.

The effectiveness of compost is very poorly understood and must not be compared with inorganic fertilizers - with half or more lost by leaching. Good compost has all the 30 or more elements needed for healthy plant life.

Applying one and one half to two tons of compost per acre on fair soil will give you more immediate benefit to the land than eight to 10 tons of cow manure and compost goes to work immediately. It takes six months for cow manure to be converted into humus. On poor soil, manure must be composted to be of any appreciable value to your land.

However, those seeding large acreage, such as through Conservation Reserve Program (CRP), availability and cost may prohibit the use of certifiable organic fertilizers. The set aside of CRP for 10 years will benefit the soil with nutrients and humus, regardless of the type of fertilizer used.

The bottom line is to test your soil and use no more fertilizer than necessary.

For those not in a U.S. Department of Agriculture program or are interested in natural fertilizers there is an alternative. The organic growers we know recommended Ohio Earth Food, Inc., 5488 Swamp St. NE, Hartville, OH 44632.

The final planning step, before planting, is selecting the type of grass or grass/legume mixture that is best suited to the site and for the wildlife species that you want. Your state Department of Natural Resources should be able to give you guidance in this area.

COOL-SEASON GRASSLAND MANAGEMENT FOR WILDLIFE

Fescue should not be used in any seeding mixture except in areas with severe erosion problems. Fescue does not attract wildlife and tends to discourage and even reduce wildlife populations.

The more common cool-season grassland grasses and legumes in Ohio and their recommended seeding rates and dates to plant are listed on next page.

Cool-Season Mixture for Wildlife		
Mixture	Lbs./Acre	Dates to Plant
-Smooth Bromegrass and Red Clover	8:8	Aug.-Sept. 15 or Mar.-Apr.
-Timothy and Red Clover	4:8	Aug.-Sept. 15 or Mar.-Apr.
-Orchardgrass and Ladino Clover or Red Clover	8:1:6	Mar.-Apr. or Aug.
-Orchardgrass and Timothy and Alsike Clover	4:2:2	Mar.-Apr.or Aug.
-Smooth Bromegrass and Timothy and Red Clover	6:2:4	Aug.-Sept. 15 or Mar.-Apr.
-Sweet Clover	10-12	Mar.15-Apr. 30
-Alfalfa	12	Mar.-May or Aug.-Sept.
-Red Clover	10	Mar.-Apr. or Aug.

Smooth Bromegrass *(Bromus inermis)*
Of all the cool-season grasses, bromegrass provides the highest quality pheasant nesting cover and provides it for a longer period of time. It competes with weeds much better than timothy or orchardgrass. Bromegrass is difficult to plant. The long, light seeds tend to lodge in the seedbox or broadcast seeders. When using a grain drill, the seed must be stirred frequently. Mixing a small amount of fertilizer or cracked corn with the seed helps it flow more freely. Oats mixed at a 50:50 ratio also improves seed flow. The oats have to be mowed off prior to heading or they impair the growth of the bromegrass.

Timothy *(Phleum pratense)*
Timothy is an excellent grass for pheasant and is equally attractive to ground nesting songbirds. We planted 50 acres of timothy mix six years ago and it's excellent cover. Over a period of time, timothy does not compete with weeds as well as bromegrass or orchardgrass, but it's easier to plant. Timothy was selected as the dominant grass on the Last Resort because our long-range plan is for normal plant

succession to occur. Once weeds invade the field, the habitat becomes less desirable for grassland nesters. These mixed fields become more desirable for rabbit, quail, and a few songbird species such as the common yellowthroat warbler. These species prefer a mixture of grasses, broadleaves, scattered briars and shrubs found in old fields.

Orchardgrass *(Dactylis glomerata)*

Orchardgrass is the best of the three grasses for the bobwhite quail but less attractive for pheasants and songbirds. Quail prefer bunch grasses like orchardgrass that have small patches of bare ground beneath. Quail are less likely to nest in dense sod forming grasses. Orchardgrass is no substitute for old-field, the preferred cover for quail. Orchardgrass is a light and fluffy seed like bromegrass and the same planting instructions apply.

Legumes

Legumes such as sweet clover, red clover and alfalfa are recommended for a short-term (less than three years) cover when seeded without a grass. They should not be considered a long-term grass cover. Legumes seeded without a grass will not persist more than a few years without frequent mowing. Weeds will quickly overtake legume-only fields. Their best use is for fields enrolled in annual cropland set-aside programs and not for long-term programs such as the Conservation Reserve Programs (CRP). They are useful in crop rotation, improving cropland by adding nitrogen and organic matter. Their deep root systems improve the soil's aeration. Of course, they provide high quality nesting cover. We have planted new areas yearly and along with our maintained trails and meadows, the legume blossoms are an excellent nectar source for butterflies and bees.

Sweet clover is the best choice for a one-year seeding. It establishes quickly and does not need mowing the first year. This clover is a biennial and will be taken over by weeds in two years. It is not as highly utilized by wildlife as alfalfa or red clover in subsequent years.

Alfalfa and red clover are high quality wildlife nesting cover and require an early mowing during the year of seeding to control weeds. Thus, no cover is provided until the second year. Always seed a grass with a legume for long-term nesting cover.

Planting

The aims of ground preparation are to provide enough moisture and nutrients and to reduce weed competition. Most frequently used equipment includes: moldboard plow to turn over heavy soils or sod; offset disks which chop and turn over trash; brushland plows for rough plowing on rocky or uneven terrain; and contour (Holt) trenchers which operate on slopes up to 45% to reduce runoff, conserve moisture and prevent erosion.

Once the soil is tested, the proper fertilizer should be selected and applied during or just before periods of active growth. Add fertilizer in early spring and summer for warm-season species. For cool-season annuals seeded in the fall, fertilize at seeding and again in midwinter. When we had our 50 acres commercially fertilized, we had them add the seed mix and apply both at the same time. Care must be taken to prevent nitrate contamination of surface water and groundwater by over fertilizing, especially on porous soil with high leaching potential.

These grasses and legumes can be planted by using either no-till or conventional methods. No-till seeding requires specialized equipment and herbicides. We do not recommend the use of any herbicide. Advice should be obtained from your local Soil Conservation Service and/or Cooperative Extension Agent when using no-till.

When using conventional seeding, undesirable competing vegetation should be eliminated and the soil pulverized by disking as often as needed. The field should be tilled to a fine, firm, weed-free, level seedbed. A simple broadcast seeding works for timothy and all legumes. The light fluffy seeds such as orchardgrass and smooth bromegrass are difficult to broadcast and should be planted with a grain drill as mentioned. Whether broadcast or drilled, the field should be firmed with a cultipacker after seeding to improve seed-soil contact.

Spring seeding should be made as early as the seedbed can be prepared. Late March and April in southern Ohio and April and early May in northern Ohio for most grasses and legumes are recommended. Summer or fall seedings should be done in August since mid-summer seedings (June-July) usually fail because of dry weather and weed competition. Seed should be placed no deeper than 1/4 of an inch into the soil. Ideally, only seed and soil contact is necessary, so do not disk the seed in, cultipack it.

Mowing

It generally takes a couple of years to establish a solid stand of grassland cover. Except for sweet clover, mowing the first year is usually a must. Weeds often flourish (especially thistle) and will out compete the new grass/legume seeding if not mowed. Mow two or three times the first year, if weeds are persistent. Spot mowing of problem areas is recommended or you will lose the first year of nesting cover.

The goal of grassland maintenance is to control weeds yet not destroy wildlife nests. To do this, only mow part of each field each year. Do not mow the entire field every year.

Many birds, especially pheasants, use grass fields as cover and roosting sites in the fall and winter. Most birds prefer to nest in the dead grasses from the previous year's growth. If the entire field is mowed each year, fewer birds will use the grassland cover the following spring for nesting.

Mowing should occur only during the first half of August, not before or after. Mowing too early causes nest destruction and too late does not allow enough time for regrowth before winter. Lack of regrowth prior to winter may cause winter-kill of grasses and legumes. Just as important, there will be insufficient winter cover for wildlife.

Summary For Cool-Season Grass Establishment

1. Select a large, open field that has moderate to good fertility and drainage, and is free of trees.
2. Soil test the field; apply lime and fertilizer adequate for grassland planting.
3. If using conventional tillage, prepare a fine, firm seedbed in March for spring seeding, late July for fall seeding.
4. Plant the seed during recommended time periods using one of the following methods:
   Broadcast method for timothy and legumes: spread seed over prepared seedbed, then cultipack field for good seed-soil contact.
   Drill method useful for all grasses and legumes: drill seed (shallow) into prepared seedbed, cultipack field.

5. If weeds flourish before the grasses and legumes become established, mow the field as many times as needed to control the weeds.
6. After the grassland is established, mow the field only when needed to control weeds. Do not mow during the nesting season. Mow from August 1 to August 15. Mow only part of the field each year.

WARM-SEASON GRASSLAND MANAGEMENT FOR WILDLIFE

Even though bromegrass, timothy, orchardgrass and red clover fields provide ideal nesting cover for pheasant, these cool-season grasses and legumes have some major drawbacks. They are usually harvested for hay or grazed by mid to late June. Many nests are destroyed and hens killed during this peak of the pheasant hatching season. Even when these cool-season grasses are planted specifically for wildlife nesting cover, they still must be mowed every two to three years to slow the invasion of weeds and trees. Eventually, the fields must be replanted to improve the quality of the grassland habitat.

Native grasses such as switchgrass, Indiangrass, and big and little bluestem are used heavily by the ring-necked pheasants and songbirds for nesting cover, winter cover and escape cover. They should out compete weeds and brush for a long period of time with minimal cost and effort and unlike cool-season grasses they don't have to be replanted.

The same fields that provide wildlife habitat can also produce cattle forage since these grasses are not hayed or grazed until after wildlife nesting season. Landowners should include warm-season grasses in their habitat plan or livestock grazing rotations because of their high quality forage after nesting season. The high quality nesting cover and long term habitat with minimal maintenance makes warm-season grassland for wildlife a necessary choice in wildlife habitat restoration. The Last Resort is now incorporating warm-season grassland habitats into the long range plan.

See next page for lists of warm-season grasses and recommended seeding rates:

Warm-Season Grasses Beneficial to Wildlife		
Species	Seeding Rate in Lbs./Acres Drilled	Broadcast
Switchgrass	6	10
Big Bluestem	10	15
Indiangrass	10	15
Little Bluestem	8	12
Mixtures*		
Switchgrass or Indiangrass and Big bluestem	1:3:6	1:6:8
Switchgrass and Indiangrass and Big bluestem and Little bluestem	1:3:3:4	1:3:5:5

*When seeding switchgrass in mixture, reduce the rate. Switchgrass will out compete the other prairie grasses if seeded too heavily.

Switchgrass *(Panicum virgatum)*

Switchgrass is a dense, sod-forming grass that will grow four to five feet tall. A number of commonly planted varieties are available in Ohio with Blackwell and Cave-In-Rock being the most common. Switchgrass provides excellent cattle forage and wildlife nesting habitat. This grass stands up well to winter snows and provides good winter cover for pheasants, song-birds, and small mammals.

Switchgrass is the easiest warm-season grass to plant because the seed is hard and small, about the size of alfalfa. The same planting method used for clover or alfalfa can be used. It is the lowest priced seed of the four warm-season grasses.

Studies indicate that switchgrass could replace corn as a source of ethanol, a fuel alcohol. Experts believe that may be possible within 10 years. There are several other environmental advantages to growing switchgrass. The grass uses less than half the nitrogen needed for corn and needs no pesticides. Once planted it requires no cultivation and very little fertilizer.

Big bluestem *(Andropogan gerardii)*
Big bluestem is a bunchgrass that grows from five to seven feet tall. It's an excellent wildlife nesting cover that also provides highly palatable and nutritious forage for cattle. Songbirds prefer this grass over other warm-season grasses. This grass tends to flatten down under heavy snows so it's poor winter cover. The seed is very light and fluffy with hairs and appendages that make it difficult to seed. It requires specialized equipment or debearding in order to plant.

Little bluestem *(Andropogan scoparius)*
Little bluestem is also a bunchgrass but only grows three to four feet and is not usually used for grazing. It is an excellent pheasant and quail nesting cover but flattens under heavy snows and is rated as poor for winter cover. The seed, similar to big bluestem, is difficult to plant.

Indiangrass *(Sorghastrum nutans)*
Indiangrass is a tall bunchgrass reaching heights of five to seven feet. It is good for grazing and wildlife habitat. Indiangrass ranks second among warm-season grasses used for songbirds and third for nesting pheasants. It stands up well to heavy snows and is a valuable winter cover. Seeding is difficult since Indiangrass seed is similar to big and little bluestem.

Mixed Prairie Grasses
The grasses provide different things for different kinds of wildlife. Some provide better winter cover and others provide better nesting cover. Quail nesting densities are highest in little bluestem. Pheasant nesting densities are highest in switchgrass and songbird nesting highest in big bluestem and Indiangrass. Switchgrass and Indiangrass provide good winter cover while big and little bluestem have little value in that respect. Planting a mixture of warm-season grasses takes advantage of each grass's best characteristics. Switchgrass and Indiangrass should be in all mixtures. A mixture of each of the four would give the greatest habitat diversity and benefit the most wildlife species.
Mixtures are not recommended for grazing. Selective grazing by cattle causes one grass species to dominate. The end result is a single species stand.

Establishment

Establishment of warm-seasoned grasses is a very slow process taking two to three years and requiring strict adherence to management guidelines. Once established, minimal maintenance is needed to retain a high quality nesting cover.

Select well drained fields of moderate fertility. Determine lime and fertilizer requirements by a soil test. Native grasses can grow and persist under poor soil fertility but a pH of 6 or higher and 25 pounds of available phosphorus (P) and potassium (K) are recommended. Nitrogen (N) applied before prairie grass establishment will stimulate competition from weeds and cool-season grasses.

Seeding Preparations - Weed Control

Because warm-season grasses do not begin to grow until late spring, it is critical to control weeds. Weeds and cool-season grasses need to be completely killed prior to seeding by preparing a fine firm seedbed.

Seeding Methods for Warm-Season Grasses

Drilling as a seeding method is recommended because less seed is used than in broadcasting. Drilling is usually more successful. Switchgrass can be planted with a conventional grass drill but the other three grasses require special drills, unless the seed has been debearded. Once debearded, they can be planted with a wide range of seeders. Debearded bluestems and Indiangrass can be broadcasted with fertilizer spreaders or other broadcast systems. The light seed can make distribution and calibration difficult.

Seeding Dates, Depth, and Soil Contact

Seed only from March through mid-May and do not seed in the fall. Place seed no deeper than 1/4 of an inch. **Only seed and soil contact is necessary. Do not disk the seed in; cultipack it.** In all broadcast seedings, cultipack before and after seeding. Loose seedbeds allow the zone of germination to dry out, causing high seed mortality.

Mowing

Mowing is a must in the year of establishment. Mow when foxtail heads are out but before it forms a seed (normally late June to early July). Mowing foxtail heads too early causes it to send up numerous new shoots. Mowing too late causes serious competition to the young grass seedlings. Raise the level of the mower to about six to eight inches or just above the warm-season grasses. Do not mow the young grass seedlings.

Stands which look poor at the end of the first year may turn out as good stands. Native grasses germinate and develop slower than cool-season perennial grasses and will only be eight to 12 inches the first year. In most first-year stands the weeds will be more evident than the grass. Full maturity can be expected by July of the second year.

Summary For Warm-Season Grass Establishment

1. Select a large, open field that is free of trees and has moderate to good fertility and drainage. It is appropriate to use native grasses around the edges of wetlands and in strips wider than 30 feet to provide winter and nesting cover for edge species such as quail.
2. Soil test the field, apply lime, phosphorous and potassium if necessary. Do not apply nitrogen until the warm-season grass stand is established. Nitrogen applied too early will favor weed and cool-season grass competition.
3. Prepare a fine, firm, seedbed in March.
4. Cultipack the seedbed.
5. Plant the seed no deeper than 1/4 of an inch deep from March to May 15. Do not fall seed.
6. Cultipack again.
7. Be patient!!

SHRUBS AND TREES

Water, food, and shelter make up all animals' habitat and are the basic needs for survival. In Ohio, water is normally available through natural sources in sufficient amounts for the wildlife. In many areas however, the food and shelter requirements of many of the animal species are not being met. As discussed in the introduction, changing land uses including industrialization, urbanization and intense farming have resulted in drastic reduction of wildlife habitat.

The restoration of the grassland habitats provides food and shelter for specific species. Others depend on habitats that consist of trees, shrubs, and vining plants. Planting for wildlife need not be a large-scale project. It may be as simple as a backyard wildlife landscaping plan **(URBAN AND BACKYARD BIRDING).** Planting for wildlife can also be as extensive as a farm-wide habitat development plan covering hundreds of acres. No matter what the size of the property, providing the habitat needs for wildlife is still the goal.

To make certain that all the habitat needs are met and that your plantings will provide maximum benefits, you should take certain steps. Proper planning, planting, and maintenance are necessary to develop an area of the most use to your wildlife. These steps will insure a landscape that will provide years of satisfaction and enjoyment and will improve with time.

More than 5,000 shrubs have been hand planted on the Last Resort within the last six years. The species planted include silky dogwood, gray dogwood, hawthorne, black-haw, American plum, hazelnut, red mulberry, paw paw, bittersweet, sassafras, buttonbush, crabapple, American dogwood and gray alder. Eight of these species were provided by the Ohio Department of Natural Resources (ODNR). At this time, ODNR no longer provides free shrubs though it is considering a cost-share program.

We still have more than 15 species of native shrubs to plant. Around here, most of the land is fall plowed and most of the fence rows removed for agriculture. The shrubs we've planted will provide badly needed food, windbreaks, and wildlife corridors for many of the Last Resort's wildlife.

Planning the Plantings

A well designed planting of woody species can provide for the food and shelter needs of wildlife. The plantings can also serve other goals that you may have. Landscaping a lawn using plants beneficial to wildlife will result in food and cover for the animals and add beauty to the yard as well.

We attract a variety of birds to our yard area by having a variety of shrubs that offer food, nectar and later fruit, shelter and perching places. Our wildlife plantings also serve as windbreaks, hedgerows, sight and sound barriers, shade, erosion control and reforestation.

What to Plant

In the early stages of our wildlife plantings, availability determined what and where we planted. Some species have specific soil and moisture requirements. However, when choosing plants for your habitat project, consider:
1. Which animals would you like to attract?
2. What animals normally occur in the area and what are their specific habitat requirements?
3. What purposes, other than wildlife habitat, will the planting serve?
4. Which plants will do well in the specific area to be planted?

The wildlife that will be attracted depends on which animals are native and the current land uses in the vicinity. Bluebirds may be plentiful in a county and a rural landowner easily attracts them. However, city lot owners in the same county may not see bluebirds in their yards because bluebirds prefer open habitats.

To attract desirable animals and to hold them, you must provide food and shelter year round. **The greater the habitat diversity the greater the diversity of wildlife you attract.**

When choosing plants, decide what other use or uses the planting might serve. Evergreen trees provide year round cover and are useful in windbreaks and in screen plantings. Some berry producing shrubs have attractive flowers and can be planted singly or in hedgerows. Nut producing hardwood trees provide shade and have timber value as well as shelter and food for wildlife. Shrubs with an extensive root system help hold soil in place. Fruit producing vines grow in areas where space is limited.

A landowner must decide whether to plant native or non-native plant species. The use of plants from either group has advantages and disadvantages.

Native Species

Advantages:
Best adapted to Ohio conditions.

Generally requires minimal maintenance.

Disadvantages:
Some species are not available at reasonable prices.

Non-Native Species

Advantages:
Most can be ordered through local nurseries at reasonable rates.

Disadvantages:
May be susceptible to disease and/or winterkill. No natural controls so may take over.

Native and non-native plants do well providing food and cover for wildlife if properly used. Generally we use native plants when planting larger acreage, especially if the area is not going to be maintained. Non-native plants should be reserved for planting smaller lots and lawn areas that are regularly maintained.

Where to Plant
We have found that where plants are located is as important as what species are planted. This fact requires that a good planting plan be developed. A general rule is to have food and shelter plants next to one another. A shrub that is loaded with berries is more likely to be used by wild animals if it is located near protective cover such as evergreen trees.

Consider the following when choosing where you plant your trees, shrubs, and vines:
1. Shade tolerance. Sun loving plants should not be planted on wooded lots.
2. Mature size of the plants. Wide spreading plants should be located away from buildings, driveways or other plants.
3. Utility easements or right-of-ways. Do not plant under or over wires, cables, pipelines, or so that any part of the plant will be on a right-of-way.
4. Soil conditions. If soils are wet and low in fertility, don't plant species that require well drained fertile sites and vice versa.
5. Plant compatibility. Plants chosen should look and grow well together. **The table, at the end of this section, presents an environmental summary of a variety of trees, shrubs and vines.**

Your layout of the plantings depends on your preferences and overall use. Random plantings look more natural but straight row plantings are easier to maintain. Straight plantings often serve as wildlife corridors. Mapping out intended plantings will let you visualize the finished project and the changes that need to be made prior to planting.

When to Plant
The plant species chosen and its size will determine when to plant. The size of stock used will depend on the amount of time and money you wish to invest and how anxious you are to see the results. Because of the many acres involved, we have used seeding stock. It has taken a few years before we began to see spectacular results. It's exciting to see all of the fall colors from our six year plantings. For the first year, we were just excited that those little twigs were surviving.

Seeding stock is generally sold as bare root stock packaging (six to 24 inches tall) having no soil included in packaging.

Plantings are made as soon as the ground thaws in the spring. In Ohio, this is during the first part of March. However, most seedling stock can be planted through the month of May.

Bare root stock that cannot be planted immediately must be "heeled in". Dig a shallow ditch. Place the planting stock in the ditch either as small bundles or a single layer. Cover the roots entirely with soil. Moisten to keep the roots from drying out. During the next few weeks, as time and/or weather permits, the stock can be removed and planted in the permanent location. The plants can't be left "heeled in" until the following year. The root system will become tangled and the young plants can't be separated without damaging the roots.

Larger stock comes with the root system surrounded by the soil in which it grew. It's either wrapped in cloth such as burlap or placed in containers. It's possible to plant more mature stock as soon as the weather starts to cool in late September until the ground freezes. We haven't had good luck with fall planting. Many of the plants heaved during the freeze and thaw of winter and spring. We recommend spring planting, March through mid May.

Where to Get Planting Stock

Trees, shrubs, and vining plants can be obtained from a variety of sources. Different government agencies make planting stock available to the landowner (either free or for a reasonable cost). Contact your state Department of Natural Resources (DNR), Soil Conservation Service (SCS), or Cooperative Extension Agent. Many carry packages for use in wildlife plantings. Look in the telephone book under county or state government offices.

Plants or seeds can be purchased from local nurseries or ordered by mail from commercial growers. Locate ones closest to your geographical area and always order from those farther north than you so that the stock will be more cold-resistant. Although many local department store garden shops carry woody plants suitable for wildlife plantings, these shrubs may have been grown in different areas and may not be accustomed to your climate.

Transplanting from wild sources is another way to get the desired plants. The drawbacks are the time involved and getting permission from the owner of the plant.

Some landowners start their own stock nursery using either seed or bare root stock. The plants are transplanted to a permanent site a year or more later after they are large enough. Plant species that are hard to establish due to grass or weed competition or eaten as seedlings by wildlife are best started in a nursery. We can't recommend this procedure for large quantities because of the time necessary for transplanting.

How to Plant Woody Plants

Proper planting techniques will help insure the survival of the young planting stock. Plants must be spaced far enough apart to prevent overcrowding but close enough to create the desired effects. After selecting the site and spacing, put the plants in the ground. You need a bucket with water and either a shovel, a mattock or a planting (dibble) bar. All of our shrubs were planted with a dibble bar, obtainable through most SCS offices.

Tractor operated planters for planting large numbers of trees and shrubs are available through most Soil Conservation Service, Divisions of Forestry, and farm implement dealers. Our experience in spring planting is that the ground is generally too wet to support the tractor and planter or too wet to pack in around the roots.

When planting bare root stock by hand, the following steps should be taken:
1. Carry seeding stock in a bucket of water. Drying of the roots will kill the seedling.
2. Make an opening that will adequately take the root system of each plant.
3. Place seedling in the ground at the same depth it grew in the nursery or 1/2 inch deeper.
4. Cover with soil.
5. Firm soil with foot.

Once the plants are in the ground, mark their location. Well-marked plants are less likely to be mowed. Individual plants can be staked using brightly painted stakes or marked with flagging tape. Commercially made marking flags are available through some of the same sources as the planting stock.

Maintaining Your Plantings

Increased plant growth and optimum production of food and shelter for wildlife can be obtained by a properly maintained wildlife planting. It's not necessary to water bare root stock, planted in the early spring. Newly planted larger stock benefit from regular watering.

Protect young plants from unwanted plant competition by mulching or mowing. We mulch whenever we can. You can use natural materials such as bark, straw, wood chips, grass clippings, leaves and garden compost. There are also unnatural materials such as plastic but if the plastic weathers and breaks down into thousands of pieces, little pieces of plastic will be around to haunt you for a long time. Commercial mulches, such as a wool mulch mat, are also available but make sure whatever you use is biodegradable. We use whatever we have available. Mulching takes time but yields faster results.

Mowing around individual plants is time consuming but it helps growth the first couple of years. Care must be taken not to damage the plants. Well marked plants are less likely to suffer injury from the mower. We hand trim. Young plants are less likely to be injured and no non-renewable source of energy is being used. (Some days we wonder if our energy is renewable.) Hand trimming still makes sense. At least it doesn't contribute to noise pollution. We find that the less noise we make doing maintenance, the more likely we are to have a close encounter with something wild.

Fertilizing young plants is not recommended. If not properly applied, fertilizers can burn plants. Fertilizers also can encourage the growth of competing vegetation. There isn't an adequate return in the form of increased growth to justify the cost of using fertilizers.

Summary

When making plantings for wildlife, keep the basic needs of food and shelter in mind. Plan the habitat development project carefully. Take care not to take on too much at one time. Develop your planting plan to cover several years. Do a little each year and then spend the rest of the time enjoying the wildlife being attracted to your property.

It's difficult to say that any one component of habitat restoration has brought us the most enjoyment. Certainly the shrub plantings are high on the list. The birds showed us how desperate they were for perches by using the shrubs before the tops could support their weight. Putting more posts around took some strain off the shrubs. By the third year, we found nests in the growing shrubs. By the fourth year, we could see the shrub corridors emerging. Shrubs are tough and can take harsh weather. Even when a shrub seems dead, new growth often sprouts from the roots.

OLD FIELD

Old fields are valuable wildlife habitat. Old fields consist of many kinds of plants furnishing key habitat components for a variety of wildlife species. The use of an old field by wildlife will change as the kinds of plants in the field change with succession. You have to manage an old field habitat to maintain the plant stages best suited for the wildlife community that you want.

Wildlife species using old field habitat types for nesting, shelter and forage include mammals such as the badger, eastern cottontail rabbit, meadow vole and red fox. Birds such as the field sparrow, American woodcock, bobwhite quail, song sparrow and American goldfinch also inhabit old field habitat, as do the monarch and eastern black swallowtail butterflies. The following numbers of each group of Ohio breeding wildlife use old field habitat: 31 mammals, 76 birds, 15 reptiles and seven amphibians.

What is Old Field Habitat?

Old field habitat is the stage of plant growth that occurs between fallow ground and forest land. Old fields are abandoned pastures and retired crop fields. They can be located both in the flooded areas along rivers and streams and in better drained areas of the uplands.

Two distinct plant stages make up an old field habitat: the meadow and the shrub stage. The meadow stage occurs in one to three year old fields. The plant succession consists of various native and naturalized grasses and forbs (a broad-leaved flowering plant). The meadow stage in an upland field includes any combination of grasses such as timothy, bromegrass, orchardgrass, bluegrass, foxtail, poverty grass and panic grass. Perennial and annual forbs found during this stage include Queen Anne's lace, lambsquarter, goldenrod, ironweed, chicory, pigweed, teasel, milkweed, daisy flea-bane, yarrow, daisies, cinquefoil, plantain, wild strawberry and black-eyed Susans.

An old field, during the process of succession, has a variety of plants. Listing the plants and animals fails to convey what an old field really is. An old field habitat is one of our favorites. You have to stand at the edge or in the middle of one to really appreciate why we're so fond of the old field habitat.

An old field illustrates the maxim, **diveristy in habitat results in diversity in wildlife.** The diversity of plants found in an old field results in a variety of animals that use the field. Our old field habitats support more birds and insects than the grass-lands do.

Meadows in bottomland old fields have different plant composition from those in adjacent uplands. Non woody (herbaceous) plants such as rushes, sedges, smartweed, reed canary grass, ragweed and barnyard grass generally appear in bottomland meadows.

Old fields, in contrast to grasslands, are comprised of 50% or more of forbs. Shrubs make up less than 10% of the stand within the meadow stage of an old field habitat. Many of the forbs that come in aren't native but then hardly anything is in Ohio. One or more flower species is always in bloom in old field habitats. Many native butterflies and birds have learned to use non-native forbs as food and shelter. During severe droughts, the non-natives furnished a constant source of nectar for butterflies. Even in years when butterflies are not common, we see butterflies in the old field.

The shrub stage develops as the meadow changes and becomes dominated by 10% or more of woody plant species, primarily seedling and sapling size. A seedling is any woody plant less than three feet tall. Those woody plants at least three feet tall, but less than 3.9 inches in diameter are saplings. If woody plants larger than four inches in diameter make up more than 50% of the canopy, the habitat cover is classified as early woodland, not old field.

A shrub stage old field good for wildlife would consist of 10% to 30% shrubs and young trees, distributed throughout the field. The ground cover is a mixture of grass and forbs. The ground cover of a shrub stage old field has herbaceous plant species similar to those found in the meadow stage but with more perennial forbs than annuals.

Upland shrubs and trees that naturally pioneer and dominate old fields include hawthorn, wild crabapple, sassafras, sumac, flowering dogwood, blackberry, raspberry, red cedar and successional hardwoods. Common successional hardwoods are ash, black walnut, honey and black locust, elm, wild black cherry, red maple, yellow poplar, aspen, shingle oak, persimmon and black oak. Other woody plants include shrubs and vines such as wild plum, blackhaw, poison ivy, redbud, shrubby St. John's wort and Japanese honeysuckle. We spend gratifying time roaming the old field, checking out the volunteers, shrubs and trees that nature planted.

Bottomland shrubs and trees include speckled or common alder, silky dogwood, gray dogwood, buttonbush and successional hardwoods. Common successional hardwoods found in bottomland areas are cottonwood, sycamore, box elder, willows, hackberry, green ash, black and honey locust, elm and silver maple. Other woody shrubs and vines such as elderberry, poison ivy, black chokeberry, highbush cranberry and prickly ash can be found in the bottomland old field habitat.

Management

There are a few methods and practices for creating, restoring and maintaining old fields that should provide you with the **best available habitat for the greatest diversity of wildlife.**

Most old fields are created when pastures and cultivated fields are abandoned and allowed to revert to natural vegetation. Maybe that is why we like old fields so much. It is **LET IT GO AND LET IT GROW.** At the Last Resort, we have a nine acre Conservation Reserve Program field that is being reforested under a plan of ODNR's Division of Forestry. The ultimate goal is the establishment of a hardwood forest through natural succession. There is enough mature woodland surrounding this acreage to seed the field. To provide the best cover, it is best to implement certain management practices.

The meadow stage old field can be established on idle pasture land by simply letting the field revert naturally. Disking strips 10 to 15 feet wide throughout the pasture will promote plant diversity, increase insect densities and furnish additional edge.

If you want a shrub type old field, let the pasture revert and native woody species will come in. You can speed the process by planting shrubs in the location and density that you desire. Conditions such as soil type, topography, exposure, moisture and geography dictate the plants occupying old fields. Refer to **Shrubs and Trees** for selecting the correct upland or bottomland species for planting your site.

Distribute the shrubs randomly throughout the pasture. It is best to mow or hand trim around the planted shrubs. As stated before, trimming reduces competition and encourages proper growth. Trimming should be continued until the shrub has reached a height greater than that of the surrounding vegetation. We trim as time and energy lets us. With our large-scale plantings, we have to be content with slower growth. A shrubby old field that has 10% to 30% woody plant density is the most productive for wildlife.

To create a meadow old field on cultivated land, select a field or part of a field that is from two to ten acres in size. Marginal farmlands make excellent old field habitats. Seed the area with a grass/legume mixture in March or August (GRASSES AND LEGUMES). A good mixture of two to three pounds of timothy and four pounds of red clover per acre provides an adequate ground cover until natural vegetation is established. Disking the field lightly prior to seeding provides a seed bed for germination. A cyclone seed broadcaster can be used for sowing the seed. Shrubs can be planted if the desired management goal is to convert the crop field to a shrub stage old field.

Restoring and Maintaining Old Fields

Restoring or maintaining old field habitat type involves periodic disturbance of the vegetation during plant succession. Natural circumstances such as fire, wind and flooding, or activities such as cultivation, mowing or cutting are disturbances which cause vegetation changes. Planned disturbances at the proper time during succession can enhance an old field for wildlife. If an old field has already advanced beyond your desired stage, you can follow a few practices to counteract succession and help revert to an earlier stage.

Released Cutting

Cutting will maintain proper woody stem densities, provide additional space for the growth of beneficial plant species and preserve plant diversity. Do not cut woody plants that produce food and supply low brush cover for wildlife. Rather, remove undesirable woody plants such as elm, ash, osage orange, maple, hackberry, box elder, yellow poplar and honey locust. Cutting is easier during the dormant season, during cooler weather and good visibility. Use a chain saw, axe or bow saw in cutting. **Construct brush piles with the cut brush.**

Brush Piles

Brush piles are a quick method to produce good ground cover. They are an excellent escape cover for many varieties of wildlife (quail, pheasant, rabbits, squirrels, songbirds). Brush piles provide excellent perches for bluebirds and other birds. Brush piles are within 10 yards of each bluebird house on all our bluebird trails.

In spite of the name, a brush pile is not just a pile of brush. If the pile doesn't have a base, the brush collapses and ceases to be escape cover.

The base of brush piles can be rot-resistant logs like oak and locust, six inches or more in diameter, or even large stumps, old fence posts, old barn beams, rolls of woven wire, large stones, metal grills supported by cinder blocks, tractor tires or old farm implements. We have used most of these quite successfully. We're recycling and using things that had been in the way. Now that old disc is supporting a brush pile.

To build a basic brush pile start with a foundation formed by crisscrossing logs in a crude log cabin fashion. This structure will support limbs and branches placed over it to a height of 10 to 15 feet. If logs are used, they should be placed parallel about four to six inches apart, with a second layer of large logs added on top at a right angle, and finally, finer woody material added in alternating layers.

A six-inch diameter tile drainpipe, two and one half feet long, added to the soil at the edge of the brush pile near an animal trail, will attract burrowing animals. Discarded Christmas trees can be stacked in clumps or along fence lines.

Brush piles, on the average, last three to five years and must have about two pickup loads of new brush added every other year to maintain an adequate cover. Brush piles should be spaced at least 200 feet apart and positioned along the edge of the field or adjacent to a food plot. We have created a wildlife corridor by using brush piles. A network of brush piles is placed in the interior of fields providing a safe travel lane for wildlife.

Wildlife deposit the seeds of their preferred foods in their droppings at the brush pile. Birds, during flight to and from the pile do the same. These seeds will germinate and in time develop into a tangled living brush pile composed of those shrubs and weeds preferred as wildlife food. **Never burn a brush pile!**

We don't own a chain saw. Brush piles were out of the question until we followed a pickup loaded with brush one day. After stopping the driver, we discovered that this tree trimmer was taking the brush to the next county to burn. After explaining that we could save him 10 miles round trip, he said that he would deliver the brush, and unload it anywhere we wanted. That was 20 brush piles ago. More than 50 loads of brush showed up that summer. More than eight different drivers learned how to construct brush piles. Over the past few years the brush piles have been refurbished by these same tree trimmers.

It's also possible to construct a living brush pile. An old field meadow that is beginning to advance to the shrub stage can be renovated by removing all existing woody vegetation and building brush piles from the cuttings. An alternative method to release cutting exists. By cutting and bending the stem of larger woody species, a horizontal brush growth will occur. These half-cuts provide cover by functioning as a living brush pile. Preferred species for half-cutting include black locust, honey locust, osage orange, red cedar and Washington hawthorn.

Cuts should be made in the spring after dormancy and when the sap is flowing. Cut halfway or twothirds of the way through the trunk at ground level being careful not to completely sever it. Next, simply push the tree to the ground. Group cuttings of three to four trees pushed and piled together creates the most effect, but single tree half-cuts provide a ready source of immediate cover.

Disking

An effective way to control unwanted woody growth and improve herbaceous plant composition is disking the old field. A heavy duty off-set or trash disc can be used to turn under small seedling-size woody stems. Exposing the root system during the winter will help kill small trees and shrubs. Follow this practice during the fall but avoid disking erosion prone areas of the field during this time of the year.

Lightly disking strips 10 to 15 feet wide in the open areas of the old field will stimulate the growth of herbaceous plants. Meander the strips throughout the field to create as much edge as possible close to protective shelter. Alternate strips every two years or until desirable vegetation is established. **Disking does increase insect population and promotes plant diversity.**

Mowing

A more traditional method of controlling undesirable vege-tation is mowing. Strip and spot mowing are the two approaches to clipping old field habitat. Strip mowing controls woody plants, develops edge, increases availability of succulent plants and improves plant composition. We have found that mowing also attracts more raptors since the mowed areas provide easier hunting. Mow strips 10 to 20 feet wide but not until after August 1.

Mowing after August 1 helps late nesters and second broods. Enough time remains for vegetation to regrow and furnish cover during the fall. Mowed strips should be at least

80 to 100 feet apart. Rotate the mowing schedule so that the same strips will be mowed only once every five to seven years.

The mowed areas will be more attractive to wildlife and people if you wind and turn the strips in a "snake-like" fashion. The turns increase the edge effect and make the mowed areas appear natural. Concentrate on the areas that are being invaded by an excessive amount of seedling size woody stems. This strip mowing will maintain an old field in the meadow stage. It should be used in shrub stage old fields as needed to maintain the correct percentage of woody stems and to improve herbaceous plant composition.

We use spot mowing as an effective way to keep noxious "weeds" in check. Spot mow when it is necessary to combat plants such as Johnson grass and Canada thistle and remember that all mowing should be completed between August 1 to August 15.

An old field habitat is a must. Diverse and interesting, the field is different depending on the season and what is in bloom. During the growing season, something is always in bloom. The sound is indescribable. It's more than a hum. Imagine thousands of different kinds of insects and birds, each with its own song. It's like an orchestra where each is playing its own song but each is in tune. Stay on maintained trails during nesting. Otherwise you may disturb the nesting birds, or worse, step on a nest.

CROPFIELD

Farming today has only a slight resemblance to the farming practices of our ancestors. To the detriment of wildlife, technological advances and improvements in crop varieties have helped intensify the environmental consequences of farming. Technology did not include wildlife in its plan to improve farming. But it is possible to farm and provide wildlife with the essential food and cover. Overall, the modifications that farmers can make to incorporate wildlife also make economic sense.

Tillage Operations

Tillage methods affect wildlife. Tillage methods include conventional or fall plowing, conservation or reduced tillage, and no-till systems. Tillage methods impact wildlife because of the amount of waste grain and crop residue left on the fields. Other areas of operations that impact wildlife are farm machinery use and pesticide application.

Fall plowing is the most devastating method of soil tillage for farm wildlife. It eliminates all wildlife cover and food. Fall plowing also drastically increases the amount of soil lost through wind and water erosion. Most agricultural researchers agree that most Ohio soils do not need to be fall plowed in preparation for spring planting. **It should only be used as a last resort.** Chisel plowing or disking can be substituted for mold board plowing.

Even farmers who insist on fall cultivation can provide wildlife with food and cover by leaving a minimum of 30 feet around the edge of the field uncultivated until spring. The crop residues and the waste grain in this uncultivated area will provide food and cover to sustain wildlife through winter conditions.

Reduced tillage describes several techniques that vary in their degrees of soil disturbance. Reduced tillage techniques such as chisel plowing, disking, ridge tillage and no-till retain crop residue and waste grain on the surface of the ground. Wildlife benefit from the cover and food. In terms of leaving habitat for wildlife, **any of these reduced tillage techniques are preferential to fall plowing.**

No-till offers the greatest benefits to wildlife because it results in the least disturbance of residual vegetation. The waste grain is available through winter and spring and into the following summer. Some birds use last year's crop residues as nesting cover. However, as in most good things, there is a serious drawback. Excessive use of pesticides (herbicides, rodenticides and/or insecticides) in no-till farming can have negative effects on wildlife. Only recommended amounts and proper application of pesticides must be used to ensure a successful crop and to protect wildlife.

Crop Rotation

Proper crop rotations reduce soil erosion, improve soil fertility, control noxious weeds and reduce susceptibility of crops to natural disasters. Crop rotations also provide diversity in food and cover for wildlife.

Some farmers plant large continuous fields of corn and soybeans year after year. This type of monoculture farming provides little diversity in terms of food and cover for preferred wildlife. In fact, monocultured crops are more susceptible to weather disasters and outbreaks of disease and pests. Fields that are continually in row crops, such as corn and soybeans, are more prone to soil erosion. These farmers may seem economically successful because they are living on the wealth of the soil. Ultimately, mining the soil leads to reduced yields and increased farming costs.

Farmers who plant a variety of crops increase the carrying capacity of their farms for wildlife. At the same time, they are improving cropland productivity. Farmers can also incorporate small grains and grass and/or clover plantings into crop rotations. These plantings help reduce soil erosion, and improve soil fertility and texture. Of course, they provide wildlife habitat.

The Soil Conservation Service (SCS) offers help to farmers interested in wildlife. The farmer should request information about crop rotations that benefit wildlife while reducing soil erosion.

Contour and Strip Cropping

Strip cropping will reduce the amount of soil eroding from the farm fields. Strips of row crops are alternated with strips of small grains such as oats or wheat, or meadow crops such as alfalfa, grass or clover. This method of breaking up big fields into strips planted in a variety of crops saves soil and increases the amount of edge available for wildlife within each field. **The more edge a field contains, the greater the number of kinds of wildlife that the cropfield can support.** Where terrain becomes hilly, strips should be planted following the contour of the land. Contouring crops helps reduce soil erosion, improving the quality of the streams. This in turn helps aquatic and terrestrial wildlife.

Cover Crops

Thirty years ago, farmers commonly had yearly, one fourth of their cropfields planted as a cover crop, referred to as a green manure or plow-down mixture. Grasses and legumes were seeded in many fields solely to be plowed back into the soil as a source of organic matter and nutrients. Other fields of red clover or timothy were first harvested for hay and then for seed. What remained was plowed under to improve the soil structure and nutrients.

Today's nutrients are synthetic. On many farms the only organic fiber entering the soil are the roots of last year's crop. It's a sad commentary on farmers' shortsightedness. **Our nation's farming practices are based on short-term profit taking instead of long term sustainability.**

Few farmers plant cover crops anymore. Cover crops of grasses and legumes are invaluable for keeping the soil fertile by providing nutrients via nitrogen fixation and through the earthworms that live on the organic matter. The organic matter also improves soil quality by improving the texture. Soils planted to frequent cover crops will be loose and alive with earthworms and other life. A far cry from the hard packed soil we see on most farms.

Left undisturbed, these same cover crops will provide wildlife with places to nest, roost, and raise their young.

Any crop ground that is temporarily or permanently out of production should always be planted with grass and/or legume cover. The cover suppresses weeds, improves soil conditions, and provides habitat for wildlife.

Harvesting Techniques

Harvesting crops can directly affect the type and number of wildlife found on a farm. A farmer choosing the right time, equipment and method for harvesting, can minimize the negative impacts of harvesting on wildlife.

Row crops such as corn and soybeans provide important food for wildlife. Waste grain left behind after harvest provides winter food except during periods of snow or ice, when grain is buried and not available to wildlife. Leave four to ten rows of crops unharvested next to protective permanent cover such as fencerows, woodlots, brushlands and wetlands. These outer rows are usually less productive anyway so the economic impact is minimal.

Many wild animals such as rabbit, pheasant and quail prefer hay fields but will also use small grain fields for nesting. Nesting occurs between the months of June and August so do not disturb the fields during this time. Oats and wheat are used by mourning doves and bobwhite quail for food and cover. Harvesting small grains at night harvests not only the grain but the roosting birds. **Harvest only during the day.**

Hay Crops

Grass, clover and alfalfa fields are important in any crop rotation. They provide forage, hay, attractive areas to nest and brood young, and they reduce soil erosion. Modern harvesting of hay, especially alfalfa, coincides with the peak nesting period for pheasants, quail and a variety of grassland

nesting songbirds. Tens of thousands of nests in Ohio are destroyed each year by haying operations. **Cutting alfalfa fields at night destroys 90-95% of the pheasant nest and broods within a field and kills 40-45% of the adult pheasants.**
To help reduce these percentages, use one or more of the following mowing practices:
1. Cut hay only during daylight hours.
2. Cut fields from the center outward, leaving the edge of the fields until last.
3. Leave a 30 to 50 foot unharvested strip around the edge of the fields, especially the edges which border on brushy or wetland areas.
4. Delay the first hay cutting, especially on hay close to good winter cover, until after July 1. Most nests hatch by the end of June.
5. Reduce mowing speeds to under three mph and use flushing bars on moving equipment.

Grass Waterways and Terraces
Grass waterways and terraces were more common when farms were small family operations. Today's large agribusiness means larger fields and larger equipment. The larger the tractor the easier it is to plow through grass waterways and the more difficult it is to stay off terrace slopes. As mentioned earlier, these practices encourage erosion. Over 68% of Ohio's croplands need some type of conservation tillage to reduce soil loss.
The value of grass waterways and terraces in erosion control is obvious. The value to wildlife is directly related to the types of grasses and legumes planted on them. Fescue, Kentucky 31 and Creeping Red are frequently used because they hold the soil and can withstand intermittent flowing water. However, fescue is a poor grass to plant for most species of wildlife. Keep fescue only on those areas where water flow will be heavy or slopes are steep. Seed the remainder of the waterway or terrace to grasses and/or legumes that provide better habitat for wildlife. Use smooth bromegrass, timothy, red clover or alfalfa. **Do not mow grass waterways and terraces until after August 1, allowing most nesters to complete their cycle.**

Field Borders and Windbreaks

Edges of fields provide some of the best habitat for wildlife. During the winter when the rest of the farm is cold and desolate, these areas provide food and cover. Field borders and windbreaks provide habitat for wildlife. If properly vegetated, these field borders and windbreaks will reduce soil erosion, conserve moisture, protect crops and livestock, trap drifting snows and provide travel lanes for both farm machinery and wildlife.

A good wildlife border contains only a few trees, preferably mast producers like plum, apple, oak, walnut, hickory or hawthorne. A good field border may or may not include a fencerow. It should consist of a variety of berry producing shrubs ranging in size from a few feet to over 15 feet high. **The greater the variety of shrub species within the fencerow the greater the diversity of food and cover for wildlife.** On each side of this shrub corridor, a five to 20 foot area of mixed grasses and legumes should be seeded. In time, this area will be invaded by a number of native annual and perennial forbs. A good wildlife border has all types of vegetation and will be from 20 to 70 feet in width.

Field Windbreaks

Along with providing food and cover for wildlife, windbreaks can reduce wind erosion, stop drifting snow, screen out undesirable sights and sounds, and protect crops, livestock and houses. Windbreaks can be as simple as several strips of tall grass dividing a large crop field. The most common type consists of two to five rows of conifers with one to two rows of adjacent shrubs.

Wildlife will begin using a new windbreak site the year it is planted and continue throughout the life of the windbreak. Conifers provide excellent winter and escape cover. Always plant one or two rows of berry producing shrubs adjacent to evergreens. Plant the shrubs on the windward side of the trees, if drifting snow is a problem. Otherwise the berry producing shrubs will be buried underneath the snow when the wildlife needs it most. Select the plants that are adapted to the planting site (SHRUBS AND TREES). Mow the windbreak only the first year or two or until the seedlings are established.

The grasses and forbs in the windbreak add to its effectiveness. They reduce winds at the ground level and provide additional food and cover for wildlife.

Idle Cropland

All or some of a cropfield may lay idle for one or more growing seasons for a number of reasons. Federal farm programs sponsored by the United States Department of Agriculture (USDA) generally have some type of cropland retirement. A landowner may take land out of production to reduce the size of the farming operation, due to crop rotation or to benefit wildlife.

The USDA may or may not require a cover crop on ground idled as part of a federal program. It is to the landowners interest to establish a cover crop for erosion control and improved soil quality. Small grains, grasses and clovers will improve soil conditions and fertility, and will control weeds and annuals. Wildlife benefit from undisturbed cover. Mow when necessary but only after August 1.

Farmers are in a position to farm sensibly, benefiting them, their descendants and wildlife. Thus practiced, farming would be a way of life again and not just an economic enterprise.

FOOD PLOTS

The three most important elements of wildlife habitat are water, shelter (cover) and food. In Ohio, water is usually available to most wild animals through the year. Shelter or cover needed for nesting, travel and loafing by wildlife varies in both quantity and quality throughout the state. In many areas there is ample shelter but not always available food for wildlife, especially during the winter when the energy demand is high to maintain body heat.

In agricultural areas where fall plowing is not common, there is usually enough waste grain to feed wildlife. However, when fall plowing is practiced or when waste grain is not next to adequate winter cover or becomes unavailable during heavy snows, food shortages can occur. Most species of farmland wildlife will not travel far from their winter cover to feed during bad weather. If food is not within 20 to 30 feet of their cover, many species will not use it even during times when they need it most.

Fruit is an important summer and fall food source. Mast, which consists of seed mainly from oak, hickory, walnut, beech, hazelnut and conifer is an important food source in late summer, fall and winter. Of the mast producers, oak is the most important because of its distribution and variety.

However, not every farm or potential wildlife area has adequate trees to produce fruit or mast. Farmers can provide food for pheasant, quail, rabbits and other wildlife by identifying good winter cover sites and changing their farm practices to provide food next to these sites.

Farming with Food plots

The simplest way to provide food for wildlife is to leave waste grain on the surface along with the crop residues. Waste grains from soybeans and corn will feed wildlife until the winter snow and ice make them unavailable. Farmers who use fall tillage can leave a 30-foot border of undisturbed crop ground at the edges of the field, adjacent to protective cover. Some of the grain will then be available to wildlife.

Better yet, leave some crops unharvested next to good winter cover. **The most important agricultural grain used by wildlife is corn.** Besides food, corn also provides an excellent cover for wildlife during late summer and winter. Corn fields that are fall plowed or clipped for silage leave nothing.

Plan to leave four to 10 rows of standing corn along the edge of a field next to brushy cover or a wetland site. Do not cultivate or spray herbicide on these wildlife rows. The annual weeds such as lambsquarter, foxtail, smartweed and common ragweeds that grow among the standing corn will add additional food and cover for wildlife. The overall yields for your field will not be measurably reduced because the outer rows (especially next to woods or tree lines) generally produce the least amount of corn. Not cultivating or harvesting this corn will save money on fuel and time.

Soybeans are less important than corn for wildlife food, but soybeans provide a high protein food for bobwhite quail and cottontail rabbits. Leave five to 10 rows of soybeans along the entire length of one or more edges of your field. Select the sides of fields that are next to woodlots, fencerows, brushlands or wetland areas. As with corn, avoid using herbicides. Allow the annual weeds to grow. Weed growth in soybeans is more important for food and cover for wildlife than it is in standing corn.

The least important agricultural crops used by wildlife for food are the small grains such as oats, wheat, barley, spelts, buckwheat, flax, clover and rye. Although only some food value is provided, small grains are better than row crops at providing cover for brood rearing, nesting and roosting. When hayfields and pastures are not available, ring-neck pheasants nest in winter wheat. Bobwhite quail feed and roost in oat fields during the fall and early winter. Leave a 15 to 30 foot strip of small grain as a food plot for your wildlife. Again, save money by not using herbicides or cultivation in these food plot areas.

Specialty Food plots

The only alternative is to plant annual grains in a food plot established specifically for the wildlife. You can use these food plots to provide preferred food for specific kinds of wildlife. Buckwheat can be planted for Canada geese and white-tailed deer; Japanese millet for waterfowl; and partridge pea or lespedeza for bobwhite quail. Consult your local wildlife agency for the appropriate species to plant for best results.

If an area lacks protective cover, the food plots should be planted in large blocks of up to several acres. Corn and/or sorghum should be the major components. The stalks and stems will serve as cover. The outer rows will protect the inner food patch from blowing snow. Thus, stalks and stems are less likely to be blown down.

Pure stands of soybeans, sorghum, millet, corn or domesticated sunflowers produce the most food. On the Last Resort, some food plots are pure stands of sorghum but **a mixture of two or more crops attract a greater variety of wildlife.**

Early seeding ensures maturity. We seed in the spring between May 1 and June 15. However, the seeding date will vary depending upon the geographic area and the combination of annual grains that you use. If you're not an experienced farmer, check with someone local who is or consult a SCS representative.

Although some food plots may be five acres, a good plot can be any size. Generally it should be no smaller than 1,000 square feet. We have one that size in our front yard. Food plots should be no larger than 1/2 acre. No more than 1/4 to 1/2 acre of food plot is needed for each 20 acres of land (except as mentioned, where protective cover is absent).

The best plots are 1/8 to 1 acre, long and narrow or irregularly shaped. Food plots and strips can be alternated with plots and strips of other vegetation to increase spatial heterogeneity and to create edge. Plant these long strips next to good winter and/or escape cover such as field borders, brushy fencerows, windbreaks, woodland edges, or wetland sites. The wider the strips the more food and cover created for wildlife.

Wildlife will use plots close to good dense cover. Select sunny sites with well-drained soils of moderate fertility. Some individuals plow and disc the sites to prepare a seed bed. The soil should be tested to determine the amount of fertilizer needed: but generally a minimum annual application of 80 pounds of 5-10-10 or 10-20-20 to each 1/4 acre food plot will suffice. Add lime if the pH is too low. As mentioned in **GRASSES AND LEGUMES,** we recommend using natural or organic fertilizer.

On the Last Resort the food plots are broadcast and lightly disced again to cover the seed. Both mixed grains and pure sorghum are broadcast. The broadcast method requires double or triple seeding rates. Light discing is used to cover the seed. Do not use herbicides or excessive cultivation on food plots. The annual weeds such as common ragweed, lambsquarter, foxtail, barnyard grass, etc. will provide seed and cover in the food plot for your wildlife. If possible, **use compost for fertilizer.** Normally, about half or more of chemical fertilizers is lost by leaching.

Pure corn food plots do best in drilled rows. To provide needed cultivation, the U.S. Soil Conservation Service recommends
drilling corn, sorghum and sunflowers in rows 22 to 42 inches
apart. For wheat, buckwheat, oats, barley, rye, flax, millets
and clovers, locally accepted drill spacing should be used.

If enough grain and weed seeds remain after the first winter
to supply wildlife through a second winter, leave the food plot
undisturbed. Establish enough food plots to allow alternate
planting between plots each year. Side by side alternate food
plots work best if you have selected the proper site to start
with.

In many states, free food plot seed packets are provided by
state agencies to the rural landowner. Most of these packets
contain seven pounds of dwarf sunflower, buckwheat, millet
and sorghum and seed up to 1/4 acre. Cost sharing for establishing food and cover for wildlife is available under the
Agricultural Conservation Program (ACP) administered by the
Agricultural Stabilization and Conservation Service (ASCS).
Check with your county ASCS office for details.

In our area, private organizations including Quails Unlimited,
local conservation clubs and Pheasants Forever provide seed,
pay you for planting and many times pay for the labor for
establishing wildlife food plots on private property. Check with
your local Wildlife District Offices for the addresses and telephone numbers of such organizations.

We have more wildlife since we added food plots. Plus, we
see more animals or their evidence. We can always find
animal tracks near or in the food plots. The food plot in our
front yard has brought us the most enjoyment. We can stand in
our living room and watch animals feeding. We've observed
species such as indigo buntings that we normally only see
away from the house. In the winter, when we're snowbound,
we can watch birds feeding in the food plot. **It's more entertaining and rewarding than a movie video.**

WOODLAND

We are surrounded by woods on and adjacent to our property; our 25 acres of mature woods represents 32% of the total Last Resort area. Counting the reforestation of nine acres of Conservation Reserve Program (CRP) under ODNR's Division of Forestry plan and counting the orchard and cabin area, one half or more of the Last Resort is in mature forest or is being reforested with hardwood. Part of the reforestation is a sugar bush of the Extra Sweet Sugar Maple variety developed by the Division of Forestry.

With about half of the Last Resort in woods or developing woods, you would think that we could sit back and watch it grow. Fifty percent is not much to crow about considering that prior to pioneer settlement 98% of Ohio's landscape was forestland. During pioneer times, trees within these virgin forests towered more than 60 feet up without a limb and possessed diameters that measured more than six feet. The Division of Forestry showed us that the oaks from which our 1840s log house was constructed had a distance of at least 52 feet to the first limb since two of the 26-foot oak logs matched end to end.

Since settlement times, Ohio has altered the woodlands by cropland conversion, residential and industrial development,

overgrazing (more damage than logging), and commercial timber harvest. Today, 26% (back from a low of 7% in the late 1940s) of Ohio's natural resource base is classified as woodland. Around 94% of this land is privately owned. Two thirds of the forestland is located in the hill country of eastern and southern Ohio. These hill country forestlands are more or less contiguous tracts broken now and then by small cropfields and some pastureland.

In western and central Ohio, forestlands consist of small woodland "islands" surrounded and separated by large expanses of cropland. These woodland islands range from five to 50 acres in size. An exception is the woodland along our creeks, streams and rivers. This woodland is discussed in the section dealing with **RIPARIAN** habitat.

When Native Americans were occupying Ohio's virgin forest, the wildlife included species such as elk and woodland bison. These species are long gone from the state but Ohio's woodlands still have a multitude of wildlife. Species from every animal class use Ohio's woodland habitat. Endangered mammals like the bobcat, Eastern woodrat and Indiana bat are dependent upon the woodland habitat for their survival.

One of the largest animal groups found using woodland habitat are the birds. Game birds like the wild turkey and ruffed grouse, the endangered sharp-shinned hawk, and a large number of songbirds inhabit Ohio's forestland. All of Ohio's 22 species of salamanders require woodland habitat sometime during their life cycle. The following animals of Ohio's breeding wildlife utilize the upland forest: 37 mammals, 63 birds, 23 reptiles, and 29 amphibians.

Identifying Forest Types

Forestland in Ohio is broken down into specific woodland types according to the dominant tree species in a stand. Dominance means that a single or pair of species make up 50% or more of the canopy or upper layer of the forest stand.

The three particular principal forest types found in Ohio are oak-hickory, beech-maple, and elm-ash. The bottomland forest type is also common in Ohio, as here at the Last Resort.

The oak-hickory forest type has a predominance of oak species such as red, black, white; and chestnut and hickories such as shagbark, pignut and bitternut. Associated trees include black walnut, white ash, basswood and black cherry.

The understory shrubs include redbud, pawpaw, wild plum, sour gum, flowering dogwood, sassafras and spicebush. The oak-hickory forest type is frequently found in the east-central, southeastern and south-central hill country regions of the state on well-drained sites.

The beech-maple forest is the second most common woodland type and occurs on the poorly-drained flatlands of southwestern, west-central, north-central and northeastern Ohio. This type of forest has large fractions of beech which are accompanied by sugar maple, red oak, white ash and white oak. Hardwood species also common include black cherry, basswood and shagbark hickory. Shrubs often in the understory include ironwood, spicebush and pawpaw.

The elm-ash forest is located predominantly in the glaciated, extreme northern and western region of the state, interspersed throughout the oak-hickory and beech-maple forests. American and red elm, white and green ash, and red and silver maple are the dominant hardwoods found in this woodland type. The most common understory species are blackhaw, prickly ash and spicebush.

A forest type that does not have a dominant tree species is successional and appears early in forest development. It consists of a mixture of hardwoods such as red elm, white ash, black cherry, red maple and black locust. The understory of successional hardwoods is made up of old field remnants like wild crab, hawthorn, sassafras and flowering dogwood.

Two deterrents to reforesting are the value of the timber and the belief that woods should be "cleaned up."

Management

A prerequisite to designing a management plant for the woodland habitat is identifying its type and age (maturity). The age of a forest is determined by the size of the stand: sapling size stand is 10 to 20 years old with trees that are at least three feet tall, but less than 3.9 inches in diameter at breast height; pole size stand is 50 to 250 years old with trees over 11 inches in diameter. Any group of trees greater than 250 years of age would be considered old growth forest. If more than 50% of the woody species in the overstory fall into one of these mentioned age class sizes, the forest would be labeled accordingly (i.e. oak-hickory type/pole size stand).

The maturity of a woodland habitat has an influence on the kinds and numbers of wildlife using it. Forests generally have six successional stages and more wildlife species are associated with some stages than with others. **Woodland management is necessary to increase species diversity.** With featured species management, forest management is adapted to meet the habitat requirements of a specific wildlife species, benefiting all wildlife species with similar overlapping habitat requirements.

During the early stages of woodland development, when the trees are sapling and pole size, wildlife such as the indigo bunting, yellow-breasted chat and rufous-sided towhee can be found using it. As the forest matures to a sawtimber stand, a different mixture of avian wildlife, such as the scarlet tanager and pileated woodpecker will replace the previous community.

Set management goals for a woodland habitat that impacts the wildlife community in a positive way.

How to establish sound management goals for your woodland habitat:
1. The potential of woodland habitat to support certain types of wildlife is influenced by its size, geographical location, and the management of the surrounding lands.
2. The forest type, age class, and density of the overstory and understory will determine the type and number of wildlife species that your woodland will attract and support.
3. A mixture of various successional stages (age classes) and forest types should be maintained in large woodland tracts.
4. Uneven-age forest containing trees of various ages support a greater diversity of wildlife that do even-age forest containing trees of the same age. Reforesting is a long-term project.
5. You should obtain as much information on the habitat requirements of the species that you want to attract as possible. You must consider the anticipated response of the wildlife community and whether your goals will provide the food, space and shelter of the wildlife population that you desire and expect.

6. As a general rule, **wildlife diversity is greatest in the immature (early successional) stands.** Mature stands, especially old growth forest, draw and sustain a unique set of wildlife. Large blocks of mature forest should be preserved! Unfortunately, the price of timber makes it attractive to landowners to "harvest" the trees.

Once you have determined the forest type and age class, identified problems and set goals, wildlife forest practices can be planned and implemented. **Woodland habitat problems that you may encounter on your property** include the following: forest fragmentation, lack of mature forest, poor tree and shrub composition, poor supply of suitable nesting cavities, lack of quality edge, overgrazing, poor timber harvest practices and conversion to other land uses. **You must address any of these problems if they occur in your woodland.**

Protecting and Creating Nesting Cavities

Natural cavities or hollows for nesting and roosting sites are used by a number of woodland animals. Cavity dwellers make up nearly 30% of all wildlife species using woodland habitat in Ohio. Some cavity nesters that are found in the Last Resort's woodlands include primary cavity excavators (species that make their own cavities such as the red-bellied woodpecker and common flicker). We hope to attract the pileated woodpecker as ours and other area woods mature. Secondary cavity users (species that depend upon primary excavators and/or natural formation for cavities) include the tufted titmouse, black-capped chickadee, raccoon, and gray and fox squirrel.

The scarcity of suitable nesting cavities is a major factor in limiting the population and diversity of woodland wildlife. Do not cut all your standing dead trees for firewood!

Cavities can be formed by natural tree decay due to age, weather, disease, and stress as well as by woodpeckers. **Trees that have died but remain standing are referred to as snags.** Leave snags that represent all possible tree species as well as a mixture of sizes. Taller snags are best. Snags are valuable to a woodland wildlife community. They supply nesting cavities, foraging perches, roosting sites, and foraging substrates for many wildlife species.

Snags support insectivorous wildlife, helping to prevent insect populations from reaching epidemic levels. **Unless snags present a safety hazard, they should not be removed from a woodland area. No matter what well-intentioned neighbors say, do not remove dead trees.** Get firewood by thinning. Maintain at least two snags six to 14 inches in dbh (diameter at breast height, 4.5 feet) per acre, four snags 14 to 18 inches dbh per acre and six snags over 18 inches dbh per acre.

Individual snags or den trees should be evenly spaced and can be created by killing trees that are six inches or greater in diameter. Select trees that are prone to forming cavities such as beech, elm, box elder, elm, cottonwood and basswood. Once the tree has been selected, use an ax and cut away a three to four-inch band of bark from around the circumference of the trunk. Eventually, the tree will die and provide cavities that would have taken years to develop.

Some wildlife species such as the wood duck and fox squirrel like to nest in live trees that have hollows. Live den trees are sometimes referred to as "wolf" trees. Wolf trees have large spreading crowns and broad trunk diameters. They have dual benefits for wildlife. They yield a bumper crop of nuts (mast) and provide a bountiful supply of cavities. Beech and sycamore make ideal wolf trees. Encourage and protect these species within your woodland area or in connecting fencerows.

It is equally important to preserve large quantities of woody ground debris such as fallen trees, slash and decaying logs and stumps. Do not "clean up" your woodland! At least two logs per acre should be retained with bark intact as well as the more deteriorated logs for wildlife habitat. These types of structures are used by woodland snakes, salamanders and turtles. Eventually they rot, returning to the soil and enriching it.

Grapevine tangles provide a food source and serve as structures to anchor nests. Leave at least 3 to 4 grapevine tangles per acre on trees. In most places, it's not difficult to leave grapevines. **Wild grapes are native and don't usually choke trees to death as invader species do.**

Man-made nesting boxes can be constructed and erected in a woodland area to supplement existing natural cavities or substitute for their absence. Refer to **POLES AND HOLES** for some ideas that apply to the woodlot habitat.

Woodland Edge Enhancement

The transitional zone that lies between the woodland border and an adjacent habitat such as cropland and meadow is called edge habitat. Edge habitat supports a diverse wildlife community. Cutting a few large trees along the edge of the woods improves the edge habitat. Cutting opens the tree canopy and lets sunlight reach the ground, stimulating the growth of brambles and shrubs. Leave hickory, oak, walnut, dogwood, hawthorn, wild plum, grapevine and other nut or fruit producing woody plants. Construct brush piles with the cut material **(OLD FIELD).**

Woodland edge development works best along the east- and south-facing edges of the woodland because brushy growth will develop faster from the increased sunlight. Also, wildlife likes the sunny spots of woodland borders, especially during the winter. Maintain a brush edge of 15 to 30 feet wide by select cutting fast growing tree species such as elm, ash and maple every five to 10 years.

On the Last Resort, we have chosen an alternative method for enhancing our woodland edge. We established a 15-foot wide shrub planting adjacent to the existing woodland edge. This was done by installing two rows of shrubs planted six feet apart and rows placed at least 10 feet from the current edge. We planted the shrub rows to the west, east, and south facing edges. We planted the following woody plants species by alternating species at four foot spacings within each row: wild plum, silky dogwood, crabapple, hawthorn, service berry and hazelnut. Blackberry and raspberry can be planted but we have found that these species move, or rather rush, in on their own. Refer to **SHRUBS AND TREES** for additional information.

Reforestation

Forest fragmentation, the isolation of woodland blocks by separating them from one another, the conversion to other land uses such as homes in woodlots and the demise of fence rows or windbreaks are major problems affecting woodland wildlife populations. **Woodland islands or patches support a poor diversity of wildlife** and exclude species such as the pileated woodpecker and wild turkey that need large blocks of unbroken woodland habitat. In order to increase the use of woodland islands by wildlife, a woody corridor can be established to link isolated woodland tracts.

These woody corridors should consist of a mixture of trees and shrubs planted within a 35 foot wide strip. It is best if the strip contains two middle rows of trees and two outer rows of shrubs. All rows should be eight feet apart and trees at 10 foot spacings within each row and shrubs at four foot spacings. We use and recommend primarily hickory and other nut tree species for the two middle rows. Washington hawthorn, wild plum, crabapple and hazelnut are excellent for the shrub rows **(SHRUBS AND TREES).**

These woody corridors will increase the overall use of woodland islands but also serve as a travel lane for wildlife species such as the cottontail rabbit and bobwhite quail. Also, these corridors will act as a wind break.

Old fields and odd areas such as irregular field corners adjacent to existing woodland tracts can be planted to trees or allowed to revert naturally in order to expand the woodland. Odd areas such as eroded areas in crop fields, bare knobs, sinkholes, sand blowouts, gullies, rockpiles, rock outcrops, borrow pits, gravel pits, pieces of good land cut off from the rest of the field by stream, drainage ditch, gully or center pivot irrigation may need little or no improvement. At least half the odd area should be in good ground cover of grasses and legumes **(GRASSES AND LEGUMES).**

These odd areas and adjacent fields can be reforested by planting tree seedlings at 8' x 10' or 10' x 10' spacings throughout the field. Plant some fruit-producing shrubs spaced three to four feet apart for nesting cover, food for songbirds and escape cover (if the shrubs are thorny). East of the Great Plains, native shrubs will often establish themselves naturally in odd areas protected from fire and grazing, and only a grass-legume mixture may need to be planted.

RIPARIAN

Identifying Riparian Habitat

Riparian habitat is the land and vegetation situated along the banks of a creek, stream or river. This habitat is often called floodplain, streamside habitat and bottomland forest. The topography is characterized by the flat or level plain look. As the name implies, a floodplain is subject to frequent seasonal flooding.

Plants associated with this habitat include deciduous trees such as silver maple, sycamore, red maple, elm, box elder, cottonwood, buckeye, willow, hackberry and river birch. Shrubs found in the understory layer or during early successional stages include bladdernut, wahoo, elderberry, buttonbush, common or black alder, spicebush, red-osier dogwood and silky dogwood. The ground cover has flowering plants such as white snakeroot, scouring rush, waterleaf, jewelweed, wingstem and nettles.

Extreme conditions are caused by the fluctuating water levels of the creeks or streams. As a result, riparian habitats are always shifting and changing in plant composition and physical structure. Thus, these habitats have a mixture of live and dead vegetation. The dead vegetation includes standing dead trees and ground cover debris, such as logs and natural litter. After spring flooding we've found plastic jugs and an occasional bowling ball, evidence of upstream humans.

Value of Riparian Habitat

The riparian habitat is one of the most diverse. Its dominant plant community is woodland but it generally has a patchwork of smaller habitats such as buttonbush thickets, temporary woods pools, cattail marshes and sedge marshes. Riparian land is very appealing to wildlife since it always provides a surface water source. Even during a severe drought pools of water remain.

The usually moist soil provides habitat for those animals that need moist soil. The woodcock finds its meals in the moist soil of a floodplain.

These habitats provide necessary travel corridors, allowing safe movement of wildlife between habitat types, thus promoting the distribution of wildlife populations. The well-worn trail adjacent to the Last Resort creek attests to this. Riparian lands provide critical connecting "access" links for wildlife between otherwise isolated habitats. These riparian habitats are often islands or oases in the midst of great deserts of cropland.

A stream is not a stream without the tree and shrub canopy. The overhanging vegetation shades the water and lowers the water temperature, improving the conditions for fish. Shade from tall vegetation provides indirect cover since fish are camouflaged by shaded waters.

The trees and shrubs also provide habitat for terrestrial insects that are food for fish. The leaves, branches and other debris in the stream channel help create pools, riffles and cover. This provides a food source and stable base for many stream channel aquatic organisms. Detritus (debris) formed from terrestrial plants is a principal source of food for aquatic invertebrates and eventually for fish. Roots in the streambank increase bank stability resulting in less soil erosion, while creating overhanging bank cover.

A healthy riparian habitat controls flooding. Stems and low growing vegetation in the floodplain retard the movement of sediment and debris floating in the flood water. The water itself is slowed. Chemicals from nonpoint sources contained in the runoff are filtered out and absorbed.

The riparian lands provide edge habitat, spread over a large area, making cover more accessible to wildlife. Two types of edges serve the needs of wildlife that use riparian lands. The interface between the stream channel and vegetated bank is used by species such as the bank swallow, kingfisher and prothonotary warbler. Cottontail rabbit and bobwhite quail use the edge formed by the merging of upland habitat, usually cropland in our area, and bottomland forest. The high numbers of live and dead trees (with nesting cavities) attract species of primary and secondary cavity users such as the pileated woodpecker, screech owl, wood duck and flying squirrel.

Riparian habitats serve as resting, feeding and staging areas for waterfowl and for songbirds during migration. In some regions, riparian habitat may provide the only available habitat for migrating birds to use.

The number of species that use the riparian habitats in Ohio include: 28 mammals, 49 birds, 16 reptiles and 14 amphibians. **Riparian habitat is one of the most productive habitats in Ohio.** The quality of habitat influences the health of the instream aquatic life.

Management: Protection and/or Restoration
The existing riparian habitats must receive protection. **In Ohio, an estimated two million acres of riparian habitat has been lost since the time of settlement.** Not unlike wetlands, these riparian lands have been misunderstood and abused.

Conversion to agricultural use, mostly for croplands and pasture, has caused most of the destruction. Instream and streamside habitat has severely been degraded by stream channel modification to "improve" cropland drainage. Meandering streams have been reduced to "straight ditches with 2:1 sloped banks." Channelization, unfortunately, removes the topsoil along with the water. Channelization does both very efficiently.

Residential and industrial development have also been responsible for the rapid decline of the riparian habitat. Trailer parks, campgrounds and recreational ball fields are often built in floodplains. Often times, floodplains are the only flat places left to build. Riparian areas need to be protected and restored. They protect our surface water supply as well as provide living places for wildlife.

It is less difficult and less costly to protect any habitat than it is to rebuild broken, degraded or destroyed habitat. For quality terrestrial habitat, a strip of at least 125 feet of trees and shrubs on each side of the water course must be maintained. A healthy aquatic community requires a minimum of 75 feet to maintain an adequate water quality.

Timber cutting, grazing, farming, road construction, and maintenance operations must pay special attention to streamside protection. A stream and its valley are an inseparable ecological unit. Intelligent management of all the resources within a riparian basin is the key to maintaining productive habitats. The adage "an ounce of prevention is worth a pound of cure" is appropriate to the streamside, with its riparian vegetation. Two elements, the streambank and the riparian vegetation, must be protected.

Even though protection is the first step in stopping the further loss of riparian habitat, it's also important to make efforts to regain some of what we have lost. This requires restoring the riparian sites that have been partially or totally destroyed.

Some sites can be reclaimed by allowing them to revert naturally. The landowner simply discontinues any practices or land uses that are hindering the development of woody plants. These include mowing, pasturing or cropping the area. Many farmers like to pasture their livestock next to the creek so they don't have to worry about water. Their gain is the downstream landowners' loss. Landowners need to think about what is best in the long-term and what is best for the larger community. What will it take to convince people that short-term gains are long-term headaches?

You can expedite the development of riparian habitat by planting bare root seedling stock of various bottomland plant species **(SHRUBS AND TREES).** Diversity and density of woody vegetation should be the aim of your riparian vegetation plan. Types of shrubs and trees should be based on site conditions such as soils and geographic location. Use native woody plants for restoring riparian habitat.

The following are recommended for streamside habitat: hardwood trees such as sweet gum, sycamore, cottonwood, green ash, box elder, hackberry and silver maple. Shrubs such as common alder, red-osier dogwood and silky dogwood are recommended. Tree seedlings should be placed at 10 foot spacings within rows positioned 10 feet apart. Intermix the shrubs with the hardwood seedlings at five foot spacings, alternating species as they are planted.

Simply plant the trees directly into the stubble trying to minimize soil disturbance so as not to encourage the growth of annual plants. Competition from existing vegetation, especially sod forming grasses, can slow and hinder riparian reestablishment but we feel strongly that the use of herbicides does more damage than good. Mowing, hand trimming around each seedling or using a wool mat may be required until the plants have overtopped the competing weed growth.

Streambanks should be planted concurrently or immediately following all activities that disturb or destroy riparian vegetation. Fast-growing grasses, legumes and forbs can be planted to give quick protection. However, slower growing plants that will eventually take over should be included. Mulching the seeding area may be necessary.

The best time to plant the trees and shrubs is in the spring between March 15 and May 1 in our area. Contact the Cooperative Extension Service for more information on planting time in your area. Refer to **SHRUBS AND TREES,** for more details on pre-planting seedling care, planting methods and post-planting maintenance. These methods can also be used to expand existing riparian strips that are too narrow to furnish quality instream or streamside habitat.

If your streambank is eroding and requires treatment, we recommend that you contact the Soil Conservation Service for advice. Practices such as dormant willow post cutting, tree revetments and tree deflectors can remedy severe bank erosion. Whether sediment is a pollutant is debatable but sediment is costly and damaging to our surface waters. Soil deposits on stream beds destroy the habitat of aquatic animals and plants. Soil particles carry phosphates and nitrates that cause algae blooms, depleting oxygen and killing fish.

Structural protection is expensive so a coordinated effort is necessary to stop streambank erosion. Streambank stabilization has a pronounced effect on the physical and chemical characteristics of the stream. Protection is expensive so a coordinated effort is necessary to stop streambank erosion.

POLES (PERCHES) AND HOLES (CAVITIES)

Poles (Perches)

The demise of the fence row and the advent of the clean look have resulted in fewer perching places for birds. Birds are resourceful and will use most anything for a perch. Dead limbs, firm treetops, snags, fence posts, fence lines, utility poles and utility lines make good perches for birds. Refer to **WOODLANDS** for how to manage snags and dead limbs to provide adequate perching sites for most birds. In open areas, you can add to and improve existing structures or build new ones to increase the available perches and roosts.

At the Last Resort, artificial perches for hawks and owls are built on used telephone poles. You can also use metal poles or trees stripped of branches. The pole or tree must be 20 to 50 feet tall, sunk at least three feet deep. For raptors, these poles should be spaced one per 25 acres in the open areas. As mentioned in **WOODLANDS,** brushpiles provide suitable perches for smaller birds.

We have had nesting kestrels in the two barn owl boxes on the north side of the barn for five years. To make the barn "user friendly" for the kestrels, we provided a perch within sight of their entrance hole. A telephone pole with crossarms was erected about 50 yards from the barn. The kestrels and other birds use it for a food exchange and perch.

Utility poles are easy to obtain. Our neighbor works for a power company and has provided us with many used telephone and electric poles. If you don't know anyone, contact your local utility company. Most utility companies with overhead lines replace the poles periodically. Since the old ones are usually soaked in creosote, the utility companies are usually glad to find a place to get rid of them.

We discovered another use for utility poles while traveling through the southern coastal states. We noticed that electric companies had set or left osprey and eagle poles next to power lines to keep the birds from roosting on the power poles. Raptors use electric poles as perches and many are electrocuted. An estimated 95% of such mortality can be prevented by correcting two percent of the electric poles. Corrective measures and design changes are improving the survival of the raptors.

Electricity in our immediate area is furnished by an electrical cooperative. When the co-op was replacing all the poles in the area, we asked if they were interested in being part of a wildlife habitat restoration project.

The first part of the project was quite simple. Instead of removing the old poles, they left them in place to be used for perching and nesting areas for screech owls and kestrels (sparrow hawks). The new pole was set and the service wires transferred. The old pole was cut to 15 feet and the nesting box was placed at 14 foot. The very top of the pole is a perch and below the perch is the nesting box. The remaining 12-foot section of the top of the pole was then placed in the ground about 10 feet from the old pole. Now we have two perches from the old pole, plus the new pole.

A 25-foot pin oak has been growing around a power pole near the house. The co-op has always trimmed the tree with great care, rather than cut it down. The nesting box plan worked so well that we left the old pole in the pin oak, cut it, and installed another screech owl nest.

An osprey nesting platform had been installed three years previously, using an old telephone pole, crossarms and inverted hardwood pallet. No osprey has nested but one has perched there for a time. We have also seen this large raptor suddenly appear over our pond near the house, fold its wings and drop out of the sky in a spectacular plunge, capture a fish and take it to a nearby snag to consume it. What a thrill!

Ospreys have not fared well in Ohio because Ohio's rivers and streams are too muddy for the ospreys to be able to catch fish. Nationally, the osprey population has been hurt by pesticide contamination. During the 1950s and 1960s, the osprey populations plummeted. When DDT was banned and the use of other harmful organochlorine pesticides was reduced, their numbers began to recover. Intensive management practices have also helped their recovery and numbers had returned to normal in the U.S. by 1985.

Ospreys are still rare in Ohio. The last nesting pair in Ohio was at Buckeye Lake in 1941 but both were shot before their eggs hatched. There have been reports of osprey attempting to nest or actually nesting. We have a nesting platform in case a pair wants to try here.

The Last Resort's bird checklist is missing the bald eagle, among a number of other habitat-sensitive birds. Getting an interior eagle to just visit the Last Resort would be great. To get a nesting pair seems a pipe dream at best.

No inland eagles have nested within the interior of Ohio since the 1960s. In 1988, a local utility donated an old 50-foot pole with crossarms that we had intended to install as an eagle perch or nesting area. The project was put on hold until there was a reason to install the eagle perch.

Last year, a pair of bald eagles was nesting in Ohio's interior. Until now, most of Ohio's eagles have nested near the shores of western Lake Erie and Sandusky Bay. We hope that the next nest will be located in our transitional zone between the lake and the interior. We are only 18 miles from Lake Erie.

Interior eagle populations may be important to the future of bald eagles throughout the Great Lakes Region because they will be influenced by different environmental factors than lake-zone eagles. Interior eagles have different habits and feeding patterns. Over the long term, lake-zone eagles could suffer reduced fertility because of residual effects of toxic contaminations within the Great Lakes. The fish that the eagles eat are contaminated. Since eagles are at the top of the food chain, the concentration of harmful chemicals could be disastrous.

We were excited when a call to the electric cooperative resulted in another cooperative effort. They agreed to get the eagle pole ready and set it on the Last Resort. Although we're not overly fond of modern life, we do like electricity. It helps to see that a necessary utility can benefit wildlife.

Holes (Cavities)

Artificial nests are used to temporarily alleviate inadequacies in the lack of snags, dens and nest trees. They are not suitable substitutes: They provide only one of the 40 uses of snags by wildlife; they may be death traps in winter; they may be death traps because predators learn to search nest boxes; they have high maintenance costs; they may lead to blowfly parasitism; they may be visually unattractive. We haven't had problems but the possibility does exist and it's important to be aware of potential problems. Do expect to have maintenance costs. Boxes must be checked frequently to catch problems such as blowfly parasitism. Boxes must be repaired and replaced when necessary.

However, in spite of the minuses, many of Ohio's wildlife species are cavity (hole) nesters and normally nest in damaged, dying or dead trees. Some make their own cavities while others move into existing hollows in trees. Natural cavities often are too few in number and in quality to provide enough nesting places. As mentioned in **WOOD-**

LANDS, trees with cavities are often the first to be cut from woodlands. They either are cut for firewood or to "improve" stands of timber. Old wooden posts which once provided nesting cavities for species like the Eastern bluebird have been removed. If the posts are replaced, it's generally with steel posts. Without nesting cavities, areas that would provide good wildlife habitat support only a limited amount of cavity dwelling wildlife.

Many species of wildlife use man-made nesting structures on the Last Resort. Some of the cavity dwellers that use our artificial structures are house wrens, bluebirds, purple martins, screech owls, wood ducks, red, fox and flying squirrels, deer mice, tree swallows, kestrels, titmouse, flickers and many others. They use these structures for nesting and also as shelters for roosting and escaping harsh weather.

The cavities lure animals into areas where they can easily be seen. On the Last Resort, photographers, artists and casual observers have spent many hours watching wild animals as they set up housekeeping and rear their young. Some people keep extensive records and band birds before the young have fledged. We keep some records but we don't band. We prefer to give the nesters privacy.

Some cavity nesters provide the added benefit of consuming nuisance insects and rodents. Tree swallows and deer mice eat insects. Kestrels and screech owls eat rodents. With our grasslands, we have an abundance of rodents.

Consider the surrounding habitats of woodland, brushland, grassland or wetland before putting up any nesting structure. Each animal has a preferred type of habitat. Gray squirrels do best in mature stands of hardwood forest with a good supply of nut trees. Bluebirds forage in open grassland where they find plenty of insects for feeding their young **(BACKYARD BIRDING).** Check a valid reference that have information on animals and their habitat requirements. Also check field guides, encyclopedias and various books available at local libraries and book stores.

If the area is suitable for certain animals but lacks natural nesting sites, you can provide the cavities. Providing cavities takes some effort and some expense for materials. Often you can use recycled wood. Providing cavities also requires a commitment. You have to be willing to take care of the boxes once they go up.

The rewards are many. You can increase bird watching opportunities by putting up bird houses **(BACKYARD BIRDING).** Bird houses can be bought or built in a variety of sizes and shapes. Illustrations of the dimensions, recommended above-ground heights, placement table and preferred habitats for a number of species of cavity nesting birds is provided at the end of this section.

All our cavity houses are made from scrap material such as old pallets, building scrap or grape crates. We also use materials other than lumber, such as sections of hollow logs and dried gourds.

When building and putting up bird houses, follow a few general rules:

1. Do not use aromatic or chemically treated lumber because the fumes can be harmful to young birds and may discourage the adults from nesting.
2. Drill ventilation and drain holes in the bird house.
3. Do not paint the houses. Houses for purple martins are an exception. They like white houses. We have read that tree swallows also like painted houses but the ones who live here do just fine in unpainted ones. If you have to paint, paint the box in the fall and let it set out to weather before spring. We let all our boxes weather.
4. Locate the houses near natural nesting habitat and away from human disturbance.
5. Do not put too many houses in a small area because many birds are territorial and will not nest close to other birds. See about bluebirds and tree swallows in **BACKYARD BIRDING.**
6. Clean houses by removing the old nesting material each winter.

OTHER CRITTERS

Deer Mouse Box

Insects may be controlled by insectivorous birds and bats. Deer mice also prey on larvae and pupae of gypsy moths in young, even-aged hardwood stands. Deer mice furnish a possible food supply for various predators. Nest boxes are five-inch cubes of 3/8 inch exterior plywood with a hinged lid and a one-inch entrance hole. We have found that the blue-bird box design works equally well for deermice. Place the deer mice box next to your hardwood stands on a gas pipe or steel fence post with the entrance hole about three feet from the ground. The entrance hole should face away from the prevailing winds (southeast in Ohio).

Gray, Fox and Flying Squirrel Nest Box

All three types of squirrels will use artificial nesting structures to raise their young, for sleeping and for protective cover year round. However, the fox squirrel does not readily use the boxes and prefers natural cavities.

A variety of materials can be used, such as nail kegs, old tires and sections of hollow logs. A wooden den box can be made from rough lumber. The three-inch hole should be on the side of the box so the hole will be near the trunk of the tree, allowing easy entry by the squirrels.

Place the squirrel box at least 30 feet above the ground in a tree at least 10 inches in diameter. The entrance hole should face away from the prevailing winds (southeast in Ohio). One to three boxes per acre will maintain a maximum squirrel population. The success of the boxes depends upon the food supply. Hardwood stands 30 to 60 years old, when cavities for squirrel are scarce but mast crops are abundant, are the best places for squirrel boxes. You'll need about 100 pounds of mast per acre so you'll probably want to identify your mast producing trees before you start building squirrel boxes.

The entrance can be lined with sheet metal to prevent gnawing. The hole can be made smaller for flying squirrels. The box can be made more enticing by partially filling it with dry leaves. Attach the box to the tree with two lag screws and washers and loosen the screws each year to allow for tree growth.

Raccoons

If, by chance, you don't have enough raccoons in your area, you can provide nesting areas. If you're having trouble with raccoons trying to live in your attic or someplace else equally obnoxious, a nesting box might entice them to leave your dwelling alone. A box similar to the squirrel den box can be used and reused by raccoons. The wooden den box should be built with slightly larger dimensions, approximately 10" x 10" x 25". A six inch entrance hole should be cut in the side of the box and placed in a wooded area the same height and location on the tree as the squirrel boxes.

Mourning Dove

Construct and install a wire cone nest, made of 1/4" or 3/8" hardware cloth. The wire should be cut with tin snips and then placed in moderate shade from six to 16 feet above the ground. There should be clearance for an easy escape. Hold the cone in place with roofing nails or staples, bending the edges down slightly after the nest is secured to the branch.

Bats

Bats are among the world's most fascinating animals. There are almost a thousand kinds. They comprise almost a fourth of all mammal species. In the United States, there are 39 species of bats and no doubt there are bats near you. Simply watch for them at dusk or around street or security lights at night.

They inhabit all but the most extreme desert and polar regions. Bats, for their size, are the world's longest lived mammal (more than 30 years). However, their highly specialized lifestyle and slow reproductive rate (usually one young per year) make adaptation to habitat changes extremely difficult. They form the largest and most vulnerable colonies of any warm-blooded animal.

The bats here live in the barn. If you don't have a barn and want to attract bats, you'll need a bat box. We have a bat box but it's mostly for display since our growing bat colony was already established in the barn.

Often visitors will turn up their noses when we mention bats. **That is until we tell them a single bat may eat up to 3,000 or more insects nightly, many of them mosquitoes.** Then we often get asked how they can attract bats. Bats make more sense than blue-light bug zappers and spray cans. We have had only two bats in the house. We were able to get them out without hurting them.

Up to 30 or more bats can live in the bat house, though some are occupied by only one or a few. Bat houses can be hung anytime but the best is fall, winter or early spring. Bats may move into your bat house within hours but a year to a year and a half is a more frequent waiting period. If the house is not occupied by the end of the second year, move it to a warmer or cooler location.

Bat houses are more likely to be occupied if sheltered from strong winds and when there are no branches or other obstructions near the entrance. Bat houses hung on the sides of buildings at heights of 10 to 15 feet have been most successful. With increasing latitude and altitude, lower temperatures require that bat boxes be oriented to receive maximum solar radiation, especially in the morning. A southeast exposure and a black roof generally works. In hot climates, plain tops and shaded sites may be preferred. Bat boxes located near a permanent source of water, especially a marsh, lake or river, are most likely to attract bats.

Barn Owl

The barn owl is the only owl in Ohio considered endangered. It derives its common name from its frequent choice of man-made structures for nesting and roosting. Installation of wooden nest boxes is an easy and effective way to enhance barn owl populations. These boxes provide a secure nesting site if located near foraging habitats like grasslands and will often be used by barn owls. The grasslands support an abundance of mice and voles, the preferred barn owl food.

The barn owl is a federally protected species. It is physically distinguished from other owls by its heart-shaped face and white-colored breast. The barn owl is a nocturnal predator and possesses extraordinary senses of sight and hearing. The barn owl screeches rather than hooting.

Although reported to be cosmopolitan in its distribution, the barn owl is rarely found outside of an area bordered by 40 degrees north and 40 degrees south latitude. Only one of the eight species have inhabited North America. Populations have declined in some areas of the United States, including Ohio. The number and distribution of barn owl nestings in an area has been related to the availability of grassland/wetland habitats and vole populations.

You can help protect and encourage this species where it still exists. First check with local bird and wildlife authorities to determine if barn owls have been recorded in your area. Look for barn owls around tree cavities, barns, silos or abandoned buildings. Barn owl pellets, the regurgitated bones and fur of owl prey, and "white-wash" littering the surfaces below an owl roost site are clues to their presence.

A barn owl box can be made from 1/2" plywood. Materials and general dimensions of the box can vary, depending upon the materials available but generally you will need: 1 bottom - 12" X 40", 2 ends - 12" X 16", 1 back - 16" X 41" and 1 top - 12-1/2" X 41".

The barn wall acts as the front of the box. Nail the box together with 7d or 8d nails. The top must be removable for cleaning. The top needs to be secured by hinges and a latch to prevent entrance by raccoons.

Mount the box on a cross beam against the inside wall of the barn. First you have to cut a 6" X 6" entrance way in the barn wall seven inches above the beam and 20 to 25 feet above the ground. This provides direct entrance from the outside. Entrance way placement is important to prevent young owls from falling out. Position the box with the entrance way two inches from one end and nail it securely to the cross beam through the bottom of the box. If the beam is too narrow, you may have to provide additional support under the box. You can also use wire extending from the lower corners of the box to the barn wall. The owls need direct access to the box so the entrance way should face an open field.

An enclosed wall-mounted box is extremely attractive to owls. Barn owls have adapted to human structures. The artificial nest boxes are better than natural sites. They are less subject to collapse. They protect the young from the weather, predators and from falling out of the nest. The nest boxes should be mounted high in barns, silos or other protected locations and should face open areas to the outside. Keep the boxes in good repair, removing old pellet material from the box. Make certain pigeons, raccoons and squirrels have not taken over the use of the nest box. Do this before nesting season; usually January or February is a good time.

Summary

Artificial nesting structures benefit wildlife and provide enjoyment to those who build and erect them. We see wild animals up close that we never saw before. Conservation clubs, scout troops, science and shop classes, and various other groups find that providing homes for wildlife is an educational and entertaining activity.

Here are some basic rules that will provide years of usefulness from the wildlife boxes:

1. Build sturdy boxes and put them up securely.
2. Locate boxes in natural habitats.
3. Avoid disturbing boxes during the nesting season.
4. Clean out and maintain the boxes annually.

The Last Resort's more than 100 nest boxes have provided habitat for a countless variety of wildlife. The boxes are work but everything worthwhile seems to require work. Being surrounded by wildlife is the reward.

Dimensions of nesting boxes for various bird species

Species	Floor of Cavity (inches)	Depth of Cavity (inches)	Entrance above Floor (inches)	Diameter of Entrance (inches)	Height above Ground* (feet)	Preferred Habitat
Barn owl	10x18	15-18	4	6	12-18	woodland
Barred owl	12x12	23	12	7x7 arch	23-30	woodland
Bewick's wren	4x4	6-8	1-6	1 - 1-1/4	6-10	near brushy areas and backyards
Bluebird	5x5	8	6	1-1/2	5-10	open field with perches backyard
Carolina wren	4x4	6-8	1-6	1-1/2	6-10	near brushy areas and backyards
Chickadee	4x4	8-10	6-8	1-1/8	6-15	woodland
Crested flycatcher	6x6	8-10	6-8	2	8-20	woodland
Downy woodpecker	4x4	9-12	6-8	1-1/4	6-20	woodland interior
Flicker	7x7	16-18	14-16	2-1/2	6-20	woodland
Hairy woodpecker	6x6	12-15	9-12	1-1/2	12-20	woodland interior
House wren	4x4	6-8	1-6	1 - 1-1/4	6-10	near bushy areas and backyards
Kestrel	8x8	12-15	9-12	3	10-30	open field
Nuthatch	4x4	8-10	6-8	1-1/4	12-20	woodland
Purple martin	6x6*	6*	1	2-1/2*	15-20	open field AWAY from trees near water
Prothonotary warbler	6x6	6	4	1-1/2	2-4	wooded streams/creeks
Phoebe	6x6	6	**	**	8-12	backyard
Red-headed woodpecker	6x6	12-15	9-12	2	12-20	woodland interior
Robin	6x8	8	**	**	6-15	woodland
Screech owl	8x8	12-15	9-12	3	10-30	woodland
Sapsucker	6x6	12-18	12-16	1-3/4	12-40	woodland
Saw-whet owl	6x6	10-12	8-10	2-1/2	12-20	woodland
Tree swallow	5x5	6	1-5	1-1/2	10-15	open fields near water
Wood duck	10x18	10-24	12-16	4	10-20	woods near water

* Many experiments show that boxes at moderate heights mostly within reach of a man on the ground are readily accepted by many birds.

** One or more sides are open.

*** These are the dimensions for one compartment. Martins nest in colonies. Therefore, martin houses should be built containing a minimum of 6 self-contained apartments.

URBAN LANDSCAPE AND BACKYARD BIRDING

Urban

Our landscapes are becoming as synthetic and false as our society. You only have to drive through the cities, suburbs and large lot country developments to see humans obsessed with controlling every aspect of their environment.

Our artificially architectured landscapes provide precious few parcels that benefit wildlife. For humans these geometric designs of marigolds or turtles and mushrooms sculptured from evergreens offer only a momentary diversion. We guess that it's interesting that humans are so clever. The manicured lawn, maintained meticulously with dangerous chemicals and impossible without the riding lawn mower mentality, is a pointed example of shortsightedness.

What a price to pay for controlling or trying to control nature. It doesn't make sense when there is an alternative. Ceramic deer and squirrel, plastic mallards and inflated air sock geese can be transformed into a lawn alive with bees, birds and butterflies. **It's the difference between controlling and enjoying.**

For all of you urban dwellers without a Last Resort, make one! Convert the areas around your house and buildings into a native wildlife refuge. **The vanishing populations of wildlife are drawn to the urban settings that furnish the proper habitats.** Using just the smallest parcel of land, you create your urban wildlife habitat. To be the caretaker of the land, to express the proper land ethic, will require you to invest money and time. Just as with the previous habitats, the long-term benefits will far outweigh the "up front" costs. Another benefit is the fact that the natural method requires less mowing and trimming, saving precious carbon fuel.

Getting Started

To get started, make a list of the animals that you can potentially attract to your area. Check the list at the end of this section. **When space is an important factor, you want to get the most for the least with little or no waste.** We wouldn't have an eagle or osprey pole if space were a consideration. We have enough space to experiment.

Birds in transit to their breeding or wintering grounds use urban areas as feeding and resting places. They renew themselves to continue their migration. Birds that winter in your area will use your area. Winter species in Ohio such as the evening grosbeak, northern junco, tree sparrow and others will frequent your feeders.

If you intend to manage your urban land to attract and increase wildlife species, you must learn their life requirements. Do an ecological study of each animal on your list. The requirements are their specific foods, space, shelter and water. Water has to be available year round. Shelter includes hiding and roosting, breeding and nesting cover.

The habitat quality and potential of your land must be evaluated. **When doing your assessment of the existing landscape, ask yourself a number of questions.** Does your current landscape measure up to the needs of your desired species and if not, what is missing? How can you improve the area? Consider factors such as soil, drainage and exposure. What are your land limitations? How can you improve these areas? Are obstacles such as power lines in certain places? Your plan must address all these questions and others that you might have if your landscape is to attract your desired wildlife species.

After thorough examination and evaluation of your property, sketch a diagram illustrating the exact location of permanent structures (house, garage, power lines) and your existing landscape features.

Form a Plan

When devising a plan, take into consideration how much space is needed for the house and other buildings. Keep in mind the amount of space that you want for recreation and other uses such as a vegetable garden. Then, decide where to place the structural (human made) and vegetative components needed to serve your targeted species of wildlife.

In designing an operational plan for your urban habitat, certain principles will help you make sound management decisions. The most obvious is deciding on the amount of money and time that you are willing to contribute.

After money and time are factored in, duplicate the natural habitat communities whenever possible. Visit natural habitats and see what you like. On your smaller scale, using the natural habitat community as a model, duplicate the plant composition and structural characteristics. Consider the height, width and density of the vegetation.

A native prairie has the characteristics that butterflies like, so if you want butterflies, investigate the make-up of this habitat. Native prairies consist primarily of tall, clump-forming grasses intermingled with an assortment of flowers of various shapes, colors and fragrances. However, management of a native prairie may require periodic burning so you must consider local laws and safety of neighbors.

The smaller the area, the more you must plan. Mistakes can be costly, especially if you invest in older planting stock. Mistakes are also time consuming. Planting in the wrong area or in the wrong conditions will not result in the growth you're hoping for. It's discouraging to have to remove something that with planning wouldn't have been there to begin with. We planted two rose of Sharons several years ago. Someone told us they were slow growing. We should have checked more thoroughly. Three years after planting and just when they began blooming, we had to remove them.

As in most habitats for wildlife, diversity is the "name of the game." Create a mosaic pattern that is attractive to a multitude of wildlife. If the conditions are present, establish a miniature marsh. Other habitat types that can be done on a small scale are meadows and mini-woodlands. Often times, these habitats can be started by simply not maintaining certain areas. When the different habitats are linked together by vegetative corridors, the corridors form dense, thorny hedgerows, thickets and windbreaks. They also provide privacy fences for the human inhabitants.

Some urban/suburban dwellers we know have been landscaping for wildlife for many years. From the street, the homes are barely visible. Most of these people suspected that their neighbors were not too happy. Often their places were referred to as that place growing up to weeds. How things change!

One of the important pluses of native vegetation is its ability to withstand harsh conditions. That's how anything survives as a species. So our urban dwellers have interesting yards without so much to mow and water. Now some of the neighbors are dropping by and asking how to get similar yards. Yards can be more than green grass, some flowers, some symmetrically trimmed bushes. They can be micro ecosystems.

The places we've seen that are most successful in attracting wildlife have harmonized natural plantings with man-made structures. It helps if the house is a natural color, green or brown. Don't repaint just to get a different color. The important point is making the whole area attractive to wildlife. We planted a trumpet vine at one edge of the house and let Virginia creeper climb another side. We are constantly being rewarded. Northern orioles visit both vines, giving us an eyeful. The vines also act as a camouflage so we're able to observe wildlife near the house without being seen.

Avoid uniform plantings and employ irregular contour planting configurations (creating additional edge) to maximize wildlife's use of your mini-habitat communities. Create as much edge as possible and don't trim around everything, except new plantings. Wildlife avoids places that are too manicured and uniform. If you have to trim your shrubbery or bushes, do so sparingly and keep a natural look in mind. Animals frequent areas where they can move about without sticking out. Remember edge, harmony and natural.

Plants, like animals, have specific habitat needs. Develop your resource list of shrubs, trees, grasses and flowers based on your soils, drainage and exposure conditions. For example, a hazelnut prefers well-drained soils and full sunlight so planting this species in a shady area with wet soils won't do. Make sure your plants are winter hardy for your climate. Losing an expensive shrub or bush to winter kill is discouraging.

Native flora are better adapted to the local and regional environmental factors. They also have ecological safeguards which keep them from spreading and displacing other native plants. Be cautious about selecting exotic plants because many become a nuisance and disrupt native ecosystems. Purple loose-strife is an excellent example of an invader that out competes the native vegetation. It is considered a nuisance plant in 30 states. Some invaders such as Queen Anne's Lace are considered a nuisance by some and desirable by others. Check around and see what the neighbors have. Also look around and see what is growing in untended areas.

Contact your County Extension Service for assistance in choosing plants suitable for your specific area. Climate and other conditions help determine if a plant is a nuisance or not. Many of the shrubs mentioned in **SHRUBS AND TREES** are suitable for any yard. Check that section for more ideas and for planting methods and procedures.

If structural components are needed to supplement the vegetative communities, refer to **HOLES AND POLES and Backyard Birding.** Erecting den boxes will increase nesting opportunities and improve the carrying capacity of your land. You can monitor trends in populations and get a general idea of how wildlife is responding to your landscape management by checking the boxes for use.

In areas with real winters, you can increase your wildlife population by making winter survival easier. As mentioned in **WOODLAND,** building brush piles provides a source of escape and winter protection in the early stages of habitat development. Brush piles can be large or small, depending on your available space. Animals need water so you need to provide a source. A birdbath is a quick solution. It serves as a source of water and a grooming center if equipped with an aeration unit or heater.

Animals need a constant food source in winter. Feeding birds is covered in more detail in the next section. Other animals need food as well. We leave ears of corn for the squirrels and raccoons. You can buy or make a hanger for hanging the corn on a tree. Consider a small version of a food plot as discussed in **FOOD PLOTS.**

Carrying out the habitat restoration plans can be a family affair. Children love to be a part of planting things and watching what they planted grow. Being part of it will instill an appreciation and respect for nature, remaining with them the rest of their lives. They can experience field biology first hand.

All the work won't be accomplished in one year. Set yearly goals, based on your resources. Don't fail to count personal energy as a resource. Just because it's affordable doesn't mean it's possible if more labor is necessary than is available. As you see your yard become a habitat you'll be encouraged to do more. Start a life list of bird species and keep a journal. **Enjoy the outdoors and have fun!**

Backyard Birding

Feeding Stations

Maintaining feeder stations is important if you want to see birds close to your house. We have nine bird feeding stations that are as entertaining to us as they are profitable to our wildlife. The location, feeder style and food type dictates the kinds of wildlife that visit each station.

If you only use one method of feeding, you exclude some birds and may make those birds more vulnerable to predation. If you scatter millet seed on the ground you will entice ground feeding birds such as white-throated sparrows and northern juncos. However, you may exclude species such as white-breasted nuthatch and tufted titmouse who feed from an elevated position.

We use a variety of feeder types such as gravity fed cylinder tube, platform, hopper box and suet feeders positioned at different levels above the ground. We offer a wide variety of foods: millet for ground feeders, black oil sunflower and thistle for finches, peanuts and suet for woodpeckers.

Position the feed stations near cover. The cover must supply perching sites and protection against bad weather and predators, both aerial and ground ones. For your enjoyment, make sure your feeders are visible from a viewing area in your home. Clean the feeders regularly and do not allow the food to become moldy and spoiled.

We maintain our stations continuously from October to April and continue enough year around to bring the birds close to the house for viewing. We like feeding in the summer because parent birds bring their fledglings to the feeders. The fledglings are awkward and quite fun to watch. The variety of stations and food minimize competition and improve the number and kinds of birds attracted to the stations.

Cats and Birding

If you have cats or if the neighborhood has a good supply of cats, you will need to take precautions. We don't have a problem with neigh-borhood cats. Cats are territor-ial and our cats, with some help, are quick to chase inter-lopers away. Not having neighborhood cats makes it easier to protect the birds.

Our cats are free fed, that is, they have food and water available all the time. Although it is true that cats hunt for reasons other than hunger, a well-fed cat is usual-ly not as desperate. Our cats can hunt rodents in the grass-lands with less effort than trying to catch prey on the wing. We don't let our cats get too trim because they are deadly hunters unless kept a little on the rotund side. We also give our cats plenty of attention because cats hunt out of boredom. Worming your cats is very important.

Of all our tactics to work with the hunting instincts of our cats, including predator guards, nothing succeeds without worming. Cats are very susceptible to worms. They pick up one type from each other. They also get tapeworms from rodents and from fleas. Wormy cats are ravenous; they never get enough to eat. They stay thin and are lean, mean killing machines. Check with your veterinarian. We purchase the medicines from our veterinarian. For tapeworms, we medicate when we see evidence. Roundworms are different. Cats usually have roundworms unless they have just been wormed. We worm periodically but always before nesting in the late spring and before heavy winter feeding. Ask your veterinarian for medication and dosages. There are natural remedies available for those who don't want to give such strong poisons.

The color of the cat helps determine how successful it is as a hunter. Tortoise shells, black with yellow blotches and almost always female, are usually good hunters. We have a half-grown tortoise shell called Kate. Kate is a dedicated hunter and extremely well camaflouged. When she is lying perfectly still, she looks like nothing more than a shadow. That is until she springs into action. She now has a pink collar with a bell on it. We have used this before with a dedicated hunter. The last cat eventually stopped stalking birds and pursued rodents. Make sure you use a collar designed for a cat and buy the correct size. Kate's collar is designed so that she can pull out of it, if she gets caught or if she figures out she can. Hopefully she'll tire of missing birds before she discovers she can slip her collar.

During the winter, when the conditions are bad, birds feed heavy in the morning and late afternoon. We keep the cats inside during those peak eating times. When the reflex of the birds is slowed by bitter cold weather, the cats have a total advantage. Keeping the cats inside evens the playing field. Ask your neighbors to cooperate if a neighbor's pet is a problem. If strays are wreaking havoc on your birds, contact the local humane officer.

Value of Birding

In expressing the importance of birding, birds could get along perfectly well without humans while we would have a difficult time adjusting to the absence of birds. Birds are important for their utilitarian and aesthetic values. Many cause damage with their feeding and fecal habits. Some that are considered pests actually help control grubs and other insects that destroy crops.

Their economic importance is indicated by the money spent to observe, feed and photograph them. In Ohio, around $126 million per year is spent in cameras, film, binoculars, bird seed and bird houses. More than $250 million per year spent on travel-related expenditures for non-game recreation. No doubt, the majority of these trips are for enjoyment of birds.

Birds have long fascinated us. A brief history of birding in Ohio would start in 1838. In that year, Kirtland compiled the first comprehensive list of 223 Ohio species, and Wheaton listed 294 species in 1882. Our latest list included 368 documented species and an additional 19 species considered to be hypothetical for the state.

Management for non-game birds has not been so extensive. In 1857, the first law in Ohio was introduced to protect sparrows, robins, bluebirds, martins, thrushes, mocking birds, swallows, redbird and catbirds. A change in status between game and non-game birds provided protection for the northern bobwhite, mourning dove, eastern meadowlark and northern flicker. In 1919 the Migratory Bird Treaty was significant in providing protection for most non-game bird species in the state.

The earlier management activities were directed at reducing damage caused by birds. In 1896 robins could be killed if they were destroying fruit or berries. In the 1930s a major effort to reduce the populations of hawks and owls was mounted in the state. Because of crop damage, aggressive attempts were made in the 1960s to control red-winged blackbirds.

Since birding is now big business, effort is being made to encourage birds. A variety of programs exist to help persons who appreciate non-game birds. These include: increased availability of planting stock, urban landscape recommendations, guidelines for bird feeding, bird trails on public areas, bird feeders to senior citizen centers and nursing homes, seed packets for hummingbird gardens, encouragement of bluebird trails. Bookstores carry many publications based on recreation and enjoyment of birds, including magazines and field guides.

More recently, intensive management efforts have been developed and initiated for some species. In Ohio, efforts to recover the barn-owl and bald eagle have been made. Efforts are also underway to provide additional habitat for grassland nesting birds.

Most of our species seem to have stable and secure populations, especially those adapted to urban-suburban areas and to brushy or edge habitats. Other species are threatened or endangered and some groups are declining. Species in Ohio (transitory, seasonal or permanent) that should be considered threatened or endangered are: American bittern, least bittern, yellow-crowned night-heron, bald eagle, northern harrier, king rail, sandhill crane, piping plover, common tern, black tern, common barn-owl, Bewick's wren, sedge wren, loggerhead shrike, golden-winged warbler, Kirtland's warbler, peregrine falcon, yellow-bellied sapsucker, winter wren, hermit thrush, magnolis warbler, Northern waterthrush, Canada warbler, dark-eyed junco and lark sparrow. Some of the birds are at risk because of conditions in their winter feeding grounds, often tropical rain forests. Birders must support, politically and economically, conservation efforts in those areas. **Closer to home, the long-term downward populations of some groups of birds are directly related to the decline in grasslands and wetlands.**

What about the future? It is estimated that 77% of Ohioans 16 years of age or older participate in some form of nonconsumptive wildlife oriented activity and most of this is oriented toward non-game birds. **The demand for restoration is high but some species will improve only if we initiate successful programs for wetlands, grasslands and old growth timber.** Some species fluctuate dramatically over time and these changes will continue. The extreme environmental conditions such as the cold winters of the late 1970s will cause some drastic responses. We cannot change the weather, but by backyard birding each of us can do our part in the maintenance and improvement of our non-game birds.

SOME BIRDS OF INTEREST

Eastern Bluebird

People have a special regard for the beautiful bluebird. It is used as a symbol of happiness or good luck and it often appears in poetry. Its looks alone would be enough to justify its existence. The male has a pleasing territorial song. Bluebirds are pleasing aesthetically to the ear and eye. Bluebirds have many other intrinsic values. These insectivorous birds provide a basis for outdoor wildlife-based recreation and have proven to be a valuable tool for teaching principles of wildlife conservation in our school systems.

The bluebird is a sparrow-size cousin of the robin living in open country, cut-over woods, orchards, fields and roadsides. The male has a dark sky-blue back and a reddish-earth chest while the female is duller in color.

Even though you may not have enough space in your backyard for bluebirds, many towns put boxes in their parks, cemeteries, schools, nursing homes, highway right-of-way and golf courses. Those with large yards or with the cooperation of their neighbors can easily establish a bluebird trail or a bluebird area. The establishment of bluebird trails is associated with many Audubon chapters. The existence of a North American Bluebird Society indicates a strong current demand for bluebirds. The current interest in establishing a bluebird trail by scouts and schools should result in increased future interest as the children mature.

We have three major bluebird trails on the Last Resort. The success of our program is evident as more than 25 bluebirds at a time have been seen on the electric wire over the organic garden. **Not only bluebirds use our bluebird boxes.** Other beneficial birds such as the house wrens, tree swallows, black-capped chickadees, white-breasted nuthatches and tufted titmice have taken up residence on the trails. It is obvious that the bluebird house can serve as a "generic" house for other birds.

We discourage the brush loving wrens by placing nest boxes at least 30 yards from the nearest bush, shrub and dense vegetation. The fiercely competitive wrens evict prior tenants by puncturing their eggs and building a stick nest on top of their furnishings. Competition is common in nature. Legally and ethically, the insect-eating wrens must be permitted to nest. Removing them just encourages them to move to another house on your trail.

House sparrows and starlings will destroy bluebird eggs and young. These European birds were introduced to North America, where they have adapted to both city and countryside. A bluebird trail that avoids buildings usually avoids house sparrows as well. Some people advocate shooting house sparrows and starlings because they are introduced species. We prefer to create habitats not favored by those species. It works!

Bluebirds raise two or three families of three to six insect-devouring young each year, from March through August. The female builds a neat cup-shaped nest of grass and lays one sky-blue egg each day for three to six days. She incubates them for two weeks and both adults feed the young for two and a half weeks. When the young leave the nest, the male teaches them to hunt while the female takes a rest or builds a new nest.

How To Establish a Bluebird Trail

Knowing the habits of bluebirds can help you bring them back to your area. Supplying nesting boxes will help restore part of their habitat. A bluebird trail is five or more bluebird nesting boxes mounted on fence posts or pipes. The boxes are spaced from 100 to 200 yard apart. The area must have low or sparse vegetation.

Bluebirds hunt food by sitting on an elevated perch and watching for grubs, caterpillars and grasshoppers in the summer. On our bluebird trails, we built a brush pile adjacent to each bluebird box.

During fall migration and on its winter range, the bluebird eats primarily wild berries. In addition to building the boxes you should also plant pokeberry, dogwood, elderberry, sumac or other shrubs to provide food **(SHRUBS AND TREES)**.

The design of a bluebird box can vary. The Peterson is the best but takes the most material and time to build. Any 3/4- or 1-inch wood may be used. Soft woods are the easiest to work with. On the Last Resort, all of our bird and animal boxes are constructed from used material, especially old pallets and grape crates. It takes only three feet of 1" x 10" white pine to make a bluebird nesting box. Three end pieces of a grape crate will construct a box.

With the exception of the Peterson, all cuts are straight and no special tools are needed. A predator guard of an extra piece of wood should be placed around the entrance hole. The added thickness makes it difficult for intruding beaks and paws to reach the nest. A **1-7/16"** entrance hole will keep starlings out. The boxes should not be painted.

Nest boxes must be in place by the second week of March and should be placed at 100-yard intervals in open areas with scattered trees. The ground should be sparse or must be mowed. Bluebird prefer the grass to be no taller than four inches. If you want bluebirds, you have to mow. Bluebirds feed heavily on insects in newly mowed grasses.

Install each box on a smooth metal post (gas pipe or fence post) at a height of about five feet and within 100 feet of a tree or brush pile. This allows a place for the adults to perch and newly fledged young to fly to for protection from predators. We have found that the bluebirds seem to utilize most those perches within 25 to 50 feet. The entrance hole should face the perch and away from the prevailing wind. In Ohio, the entrance hole should face the southeast.

Poorly or improperly maintained nest boxes are harmful to bluebirds and other cavity nesting wildlife. All nesting boxes must be checked throughout the nesting season from April to mid-August. After the young have left, remove the old nesting material to encourage use by bluebirds. If not cleaned, the pair may build a second or third nest on top of the previous nest. This practice is believed to promote blowfly infestations. Building on the previous nest does make the nest closer to the entrance hole and thus more susceptible to predators.

Even though we normally use no pesticides, a light dusting of the empty box with a 1% concentration of powdered rotenone will help reduce blowfly, spider and mite infestation. Rotenone can be found at lawn and garden supply stores. This natural insecticide is obtained from the roots of certain plants and will dissipate within hours. Read the label carefully and use proper application methods.

The predator guard around the entrance hole needs to be supplemented with something on the pipe or post. You can use a length of PVC plastic over the post or use automotive grease to discourage predators. You can also purchase predator guards.

As soon as the last brood has left, clean out the old nest to improve chances that the boxes will be used for escaping bad weather in the winter. To discourage the use of the boxes in the winter by deer mice, you can leave the sides or front slightly ajar. We provide boxes specific for the mice. Some boxes get used by mice anyway. They're stubborn about moving back in after eviction and they'll run bluebirds off. Check your boxes periodically during the winter to keep mice out.

Again, to reduce competition from house sparrows, place the nest box at least 100 yards away from buildings. The color white on boxes attracts house sparrows and tree swallows so avoid white paint (unless wanting to attract tree swallows). Because of the wetlands, we get tree swallows anyway. Keeping the boxes away from shrubs and trees will reduce competition from house wrens.

Tree swallows are superb competitors for habitat near water. They will drive off a pair of bluebirds. To reduce competition from tree swallows, put up two boxes 15 feet apart and 100 yards between pairs. The tree swallows can nest in one box. Since tree swallows will not nest close to other tree swallows, one box is left free for bluebirds. If the entrance hole is no larger than 1-7/16", starlings cannot get in. If you do not get a bluebird pair in every box, don't get discouraged. Careful placement, monitoring and maintenance of the box will increase your chances of attracting bluebirds.

Hummingbirds

We have found that attracting hummingbirds to our yard is an enjoyable experience and a fascinating hobby. A hummingbird garden takes a year or so to become well established. By planting annuals along with perennials and bushes, you can hasten the results.

The ruby-throated hummingbird is the only species that lives east of the Mississippi but the same management practices apply to the western species. The hummingbird is about three inches long and weighs only a few ounces. The ruby-throated has an iridescent green back and white underside and the male has a flaming ruby-red throat. The flight of the hummingbird is considered its most fascinating characteristic, with the wings beating from 50 to 75 times per second. These nature's helicopters move forward, backward, up, down and around or just hover. We think the hummingbird's most fascinating characteristic is its incredible fasciation with us. These little birds will hover right in front of our faces. They inspect anything red so it's fun to wear a red hat or shirt and thereby have a close encounter with a bird that more closely resembles a miniature helicopter.

Red tubular flowers are the key to attracting hummingbirds to your backyard. Orange, pink and red/white combination flowers work well. Popular plants include scarlet bergamot, red azalea, columbine, trumpet creeper, dahlias, gladioli, coral bells, cardinal flower, clematis, Mexican sunflowers (tithonia), spiderflower (cleome), catchfly, scarlet runner bean and flowering tobacco. They also visit impatiens, scarlet sage, pink and red petunias and geraniums.

We have different combinations of flowers different years, depending on how much time we have to put in our annuals. Most of our hummingbird gardens contain the bright orange Mexican sunflowers that reach about four feet high. We collect the dried heads each year to use the following year. In the same area we plant the 1-foot catchfly and the five foot spider flower that resow themselves each year.

Plant your garden in a sunny location in early to midMay, covering the seeds with 1/4 inch of soil. Most newly planted seeds and then seedlings need to be kept moist so plan on doing some watering. It's really worth it to have some perennials that are self sufficient after the first year.

We have trumpet vine and honeysuckle planted in several areas. These plants have enticed both the "hummer" and Northern Oriole to within inches of our windows. We also have a weigelia which blossoms about the same time as the hummingbirds arrive in May. They prefer these blossoms to the feeders.

Although natural sources of nectar are preferable, sometimes none or not enough is available. Hummingbird feeders are an excellent way to supplement the nectar source. These special feeders can be purchased in garden centers, outdoor stores and many other places.

The nectar (feed) can be made by boiling one part sugar with four parts water for a few minutes to retard fermentation. Honey should never be used. Red food coloring may be added but is not necessary if the feeder is red. Every three days the feeder must be cleaned and filled with a new supply of nectar, which can be stored in the refrigerator. Hang the feeder where it will be in the shade most of the day.

A commercial feed is available which we have used when we are rushed for time. It's more costly but does seem to resist mold better. If you see black stuff on the feeders, clean them immediately. The black stuff is mold and is dangerous to hummers.

OTHER INTERESTING WILDLIFE

Butterfly Garden

Planting a hummingbird garden also attracts butterflies. We see as many butterflies as hummers on the Mexican sunflowers. Butterflies are attracted to wildflowers as well as cultivated annuals and perennials that are a good supply of nectar. A large-petaled blossom provides a landing platform. Butterflies prefer purple flowers, then yellow, pink, orange and finally white.

Some cultivated annuals that attract species such as tiger swallowtails, monarchs, viceroys, painted ladies, hairstreaks, blues, sulfurs and fritillaries are alyssum, calendula, cosmos, marigold, scabiosa, verbena and zinnia. When given choice, our butterflies prefer old-fashioned zinnias. Some cultivated perennials that will attract butterflies year after year are arabis, butterfly weed, daisy, catmint, phlox and primrose.

Wildflowers found in urban and suburban areas that are excellent butterfly attractors include boneset, dandelion, Queen Anne's lace, goldenrod, milkweed, thistle, clovers, yarrow and New England aster. These wildflowers will grow well if you stop mowing some lawn space. Wildflowers are usually more resistant to extreme weather conditions and disease, providing a more reliable source of nectar. You'll save the time and money associated with mowing and you'll see butterflies.

By mixing with or planting a butterfly garden beside your hummingbird garden, you can easily double your pleasure. For both hummingbirds and butterflies, having a continuous source of nectar is very important. Choose flowers that bloom all summer or in sequence so that a constant source of nectar is available.

If you are really serious about habitat for butterflies, you want to do more than just supply sources of nectar. You need a food supply for the caterpiller stage or stages, depending on how many species you can hope to sustain. Because we have so many wildflowers, natural and naturalized, we have food for most of the caterpillers without planting anything extra. We did plant pawpaws but that was for food for us with food for a caterpiller as an afterthought. Moths and butterflies are at considerable risk. Sprays that kill undesirable moths are not usually specific to that moth. Moths and butterflies need places where they can live and reproduce safe from insecticides.

SPECIAL AREAS

Roadsides for Wildlife

Almost everyone living in a suburban or farm setting has a roadside. Wildlife researchers have determined that state roadsides average six acres per mile and county and township roadsides average three acres per mile. We are talking about the right-of-way, not necessarily the tiny strip left after the farmer has finished plowing. Wildlife use of a roadside depends upon its width and the way it is managed. Narrow roadsides that are mowed during the nesting season (July 15) receive the least use while wide roadsides of eight feet or more that

have proper vegetation and remain unmowed until late July receive the most use.

Researchers found an average of 2.5 wildlife nests per mile of unmowed roadside here in glaciated Ohio. They also determined that 91% of the state roadsides and 83% of the county and township roadsides are suitable for wildlife production.

By working with your township trustees to delay mowing and to reseed the roadsides, critical habitat for the pheasants and other grassland nesting wildlife can be established. At a minimum, do not mow your roadside right-of-way. Research throughout the Midwest has found that delayed mowing and reseeding does not lead to more road kills. Further, the grass and legume cover will actually help control noxious weeds. Not mowing saves money and is more pleasing to the eye if we'd just get over the notion that mowed is beautiful.

You might also have to work with your neighbors if they are close. They can't make you mow as long as you control noxious weeds but it's always best to get along. We handed out flyers about the value of roadsides as habitat. At least the neighbors knew we had stopped mowing for a purpose and not because we had forgotten to mow or were being lazy. We like the looks of the unmowed, rural roadside. Not mowing saves money now and precious carbon fuel for future generations.

WILDLIFE ATTRACTED TO URBAN AND SUBURBAN LANDSCAPES

Mammals

Opossum
Eastern cottontail
Eastern chipmunk
Thirteen-lined
   ground squirrel
Gray squirrel
Raccoon

Reptiles and Amphibians

Eastern box turtle
Fence lizard
Eastern garter snake
American toad
Northern spring peeper

Birds

Blue Jay
House wren
Common flicker
Chickadee
Gray catbird
American robin
Northern cardina
Song sparrow
Mourning dove
Ruby-throated
hummingbird
Downy woodpecker
Northern mockingbird
Brown thrasher
Yellow warbler
Chipping sparrow
Common grackle

Butterflies

Monarch
Black swallowtail
Common sulfur
Question mark
Painted lady
Great spangled
   fritillary
Tiger swallowtail
Silver-spotted
   skipper

COMMON AND SCIENTIFIC NAMES

ANIMALS IN GENERAL

Common name*   **Scientific name**

* denotes Ohio's endangered species

Common name	Scientific name
American coot	*Fulica americana*
Beaver	*Castor canadensis*
Blue-winged teal	*Anas discors*
Bufflehead	*Bucephala albeola*
Canada goose	*Branta canadensis*
Canvasback	*Aythya valisineria*
Common snipe	*Capella gallinago*
Deer	*Odocoileus spp.*
Double-crested cormorant	*Phalacrocorax auritus*
Gadwall	*Anas strepera*
Great blue heron	*Ardea herodias*
Green-winged teal	*Anas carolinensis*
Hooded merganser	*Lophodytes cucullatus*
Kestrel	*Falco sparverius*
Lesser yellowlegs	*Totanus flavipes*
Mallard	*Anas platyrhynchos*
Muskrat	*Ondatra zibethica*
Otter	*Lutra canadensis*
Pintail	*Anas acuta*
Rabbit	*Sylvilagus spp.*
Raccoon	*Procyon lotor*
Redhead	*Aythya americana*
Shoveler	*Spatula clypeata*
Sora	*Porzana carolina*
Starling	*Sturnus vulgaris*
Yellow-crowned night heron	*Nyctanassa violacea*
Wood duck	*Aix sponsa*

PLANTS IN GENERAL

Common name	Scientific name
Ash	*Fraxinus spp.*
Aster	*Aster spp.*
Arrowhead	*Sagittaria latifolia*
Beech	*Fagus grandifolia*
Birch	*Betula spp.*
Black gum	*Nyssa sylvatica*
Black locust	*Robinia pseudo-acacia*
Boxelder	*Acer negundo*
Bur marigold	*Megalodonta beckii*
Burreed	*Sparganium americanum*
Buttonbush	*Cephalanthus occidentalis*
Cattail	*Typha spp.*
Coontail	*Ceratophyllum demersum*
Duckpotato	*Sagittaria spp.*
Duckweed	*Lemna spp.*
Eelgrass	*Zostera marina*
Elm	*Ulmus spp.*
Hackberry	*Celtis occidentalis*
Hickory	*Carya spp.*
Honey locust	*Gleditsia triacanthos*
Japanese millet	*Echinochloa frumentacea*
Milfoil	*Myriophyllum spp.*
Muskgrass	*Chara spp.*
Oak	*Quercus spp.*
Pickerelweed	*Pontederia cordata*
Pin oak	*Quercus palustris*
Pine	*Pinus spp.*
Purple loose-strife	*Lythrum salicaria*
Sand-bar willow	*Salix interior*
Sedge	*Carex spp.*
Small duckweed	*Lemna minor*
Smartweeds	*Polygonum spp.*
Soft maple	*Acer rubrum*
Sphagnum	*Sphagnum spp.*
Spatterdock	*Nuphar spp.*
Spikerushes	*Eleocharis spp.*
Sticktight	*Bidens spp.*
Swamp chestnut oak	*Quercus michauxii*
Swamp milkweed	*Asclepias incarnata*
Swamp white oak	*Quercus bicolor*

Common name	Scientific name
Sweet flag	*Acorus calamus*
Sweet gum	*Liquidambar styraciflua*
Sycamore	*Platanus occidentalis*
Watercress	*Nasturtium officinale*
Waterlily	*Nymphea odorata*
Waterweed	*Anacharis canadensis*
Water oak	*Quercus nigra*
Water parsnip	*Sium suave*
Wild rice	*Zizania aquatica*
Wild millets	*Echinochloa spp.*
Willow	*Salix spp.*
White water lily	*Nymphaea spp.*
Yellow clover	*Melilotus officinalis*
Yellow popular	*Liriodendron tulipifera*
Yellow water lily	*Nymphaea spp.*

MAMMALS

Bobcat*	*Felis rufus*
Cottontail	*Sylvilagus floridanus*
Deermouse	*Peromyscus maniculatus*
Eastern chipmunk	*Tamias striatus*
Eastern woodrat*	*Neotoma floridana*
Elk	*Cervus elaphuus*
Flying squirrel	*Glaucomys spp.*
Fox squirrel	*Sciurus niger*
Gray squirrel	*Sciurus carolinensis*
Ground squirrel- 13 lined	*Citellus tridecemlineatus*
Hoary bat	*Lasiurus cinereus*
Indiana bat*	*Myotis sodalis*
Least weasel	*Mustela rixosa*
Moose	*Alces alces*
Muskrat	*Ondatra zibethicus*
Northern flying squirrel	*Glaucomys sabrinus*
Opossum	*Didelphis masupialis*
Raccoon	*Procyon lotor*
Red squirrel	*Tamiasciurus hudsonicus*
River otter*	*Lutra canadensis*
Skunk, striped	*Mephitis mephitis*
Weasel	*Mustela spp.*
White-tailed deer	*Odocoileus virginianus*
Woodchuck	*Marmota monax*

BIRDS

Common name	Scientific name
American bittern*	Botaurus lentiginosus
American goldfinch	Carduelis tristis
American robin	Turdus migratorius
Bald eagle*	Haliaeetus leucocephalus
Bank swallow	Riparia riparia
Barn owl*	Tyto alba
Barn swallow	Hirundo rustica
Bewick's wren*	Thryomanes bewickii
Bluebird	Sialia sialis
Black tern*	Chlidonias niger
Blue jay	Cyanocitta cristata
Bobwhite quail	Colinus virginianus
Browwn thrasher	Toxostoma rufum
Canada warbler*	Wilsonia canadensis
Carolina wren	Thryothorus ludovicianus
Cedar waxwing	Bombycilla cedrorum
Chicadee	Parus atricapillus
Chipping sparroww	Spizella passerina
Common flicker	Colaptes auratus
Common nighthawk	Chordeiles miror
Common tern*	Sterna hirundo
Crested flycatcher	Myiarchus crinitus
Dark-eyed junco*	Junco hyemalis
Downy woodpecker	Picoides pubescens
Dusky flycatcher	Empidonax oberholseri
Evening grosbeak	Hesperiphona vespartina
Flicker	Colaptes spp.
Golden-crowned kinglet	Regulus satrapa
Golden-winged warbler*	Vermivora chrysoptera
Goshawk	Accipiter gentilis
Gray catbird	Dumetella carolinensis
Great blue heron	Ardea herodias
Great horned owl	Bubo virginianus
Hairy woodpecker	Picoides villosus
Hermit thrush*	Catharus guttatus
House finch	Carpodacus mexicanus
House wren	Troglodytes aedon
Hummingbird-ruby-throated	Archilochus colubris
Kentucky warbler	Oporornis formosus

Common name	Scientific name
Kestrel	*Falco sparverius*
Killdeer	*Chardrius vociferus*
Kirtland's warbler*	*Dendroica kirtlandii*
King rail*	*Rallus elegans*
Lark sparrow*	*Chondestes grammacus*
Least bittern*	*Ixobrychus exilis*
Lincoln's sparrow	*Melospiza lincolnii*
Loggerhead shrike*	*Lanius ludovicianus*
Magnolia warbler*	*Dendroica magnolia*
Mourning dove	*Zenaida macroura*
Northern cardinal	*Richmondena cardinalis*
Northern harrier*	*Circus cyaneus*
Northern mockingbird	*Mimus polyglottos*
Northern oriole	*Icterus galbula*
Northern waterthrush*	*Seiurus noveboracensis*
Nuthatch	*Sitta spp.*
Osprey	*Pandion haliaetus*
Peregrine falcon*	*Falco peregrinus*
Pheasant	*Phasianus colchicus*
Phoebe	*Sayornis phoebe*
Pileated woodpecker	*Dryocopus pileatus*
Piping plover*	*Charadrius melodus*
Prothonotary warbler	*Prothonotaria citrea*
Purple martin	*Progne subis*
Red-bellied woodpecker	*Melanerpes carolinus*
Red-breasted nuthatch	*Sitta canadensis*
Red-headed woodpecker	*Melanerpes erythrocephalus*
Red-tailed hawk	*Buteo jamaicensis*
Robin	*Turdus migratorius*
Ruffed grouse	*Bonasa umbellus*
Sandhill crane*	*Grus canadensis*
Saw-whet owl	*Aegolius acadicus*
Screech owl	*Otus asio*
Sedge wren*	*Cistothorus platensis*
Song sparrow	*Melospiza melodia*
Sparrow hawk	*Falco sparverius*
Starling	*Sturnus vulgaris*
Swainson's thrush	*Catharus ustulatus*
Titmouse	*Parus bicolor*
Tree swallow	*Iridoprocne bicolor*
Turkey	*Meleagris gallopavo*

Common name	Scientific name
Winter wren*	*Troglodytes troglodytes*
Wood duck	*Aix sponsa*
Yellow-bellied sap sucker*	*Sphyrapicus varius*
Yellow-breasted chat	*Icteria virens*
Yellow-crowned night heron*	*Nyctanassa violacea*
Yellow-rumped warbler	*Dendroica coronata*

REPTILES AND AMPHIBIANS

American toad	*Bufo terrestris*
Eastern box turtle	*Terrapene carolina*
Eastern garter snake	*Thamnophis sirtalis*
Fence lizard	*Sceloporus undulatus*
Northern spring peeper	*Hyla crucifer*

BUTTERFLIES

Black swallowtail	*Papilio asterius*
Common blue	*Celastrina ladon*
Common sulfur	*Colias philodice*
Fritillary	*Euphydryas spp.*
Gray hairstreak	*Strymon melinus*
Monarch	*Danaus plexippus*
Painted lady	*Vanessa cardui*
Silver-spotted skipper	*Epargyreus clarus*
Tiger swallowtail	*Papilio glaucus*
Question mark	*Polygonia spp.*
Viceroy	*Limenitis archippus*

TREES

Alpine fir	*Abies lasiocarpa*
American basswood	*Tilia americana*
American beech	*Fagus grandifolia*
American chestnus	*Castancea dentata*
American elm	*Ulmus americana*
American sycamore	*Platanus occidentalis*
Bald cypress	*Taxodium distichum*
Basswood	*Tilia americana*
Bitternut hickory	*Carya cordiformis*

Common name	Scientific name
Black cherry	*Prunus serotina*
Black locust	*Robinia pseudoacacia*
Black oak	*Quercus marilandica*
Black spruce	*Picea mariana*
Box elder	*Acer nequndo*
Bur oak	*Quercus macrocarpa*
Butternut	*Juglans cinerea*
Chestnut oak	*Quercus prinus*
Douglas-fir	*Pseudotsuga menziesii*
Eastern cottonwood	*Populus deltoides*
Eastern hemlock	*Tsuga canadensis*
Elm	*Ulmus spp.*
Gambel oak	*Quercus gambelii*
Green ash	*Fraxinus pennsylvanica*
Honey locust	*Gleditsia triacanthos*
Northern red oak	*Quercus rubra*
Norway maple	*Acer platanois*
Oak	*Quercus spp.*
Ohio buckeye	*Aesculus glabra*
Pignut	*Carya spp.*
Pin oak	*Quercus palustris*
Pine	*Pinus spp.*
Red maple	*Acer rubrum*
Red oad	*Quercus rubra*
Scarlet oak	*Quercus coccinea*
Shagbark hickory	*Carya ovata*
Silver maple	*Acer saccharinum*
Sugar maple	*Acer saccharum*
Swamp white oak	*Quercus bicolor*
Sweetgum	*Liquidambar styraciflua*
Tuliptree	*Liriodendron tulipera*
Walnut	*Juglans spp.*
Water oak	*Quercus nigra*
White ash	*Fraxinus americana*
White birch	*Betula papyrifera*
White cedar	*Thuja occidentalis*
White mulberry	*Morus alba*
White oak	*Ouercus alba*
White pine	*Pinus strobus*
Wild black cherry	*Prunus serotina*
Willow oak	*Quercus phellos*

SHRUBS, SMALL TREES AND VINES

Alder, common	*Alnus serrulata*
Alder, speckled	*Alnus rugos*
Arrowwood	*Viburnum recognitum*
Bayberry	*Myrica pensylvanica*
Bitter nightshade (vine)	*Solanum dulcamara*
Bittersweet (vine)	*Celastrus scandens*
Blackberry	*Rubus spp.*
Blackhaw	*Viburnum prunifolium*
Black huckleberry	*Gaylussacia baccata*
Bluebeech (Ironwood)	*Carpinusi caroliniana*
Blueberry	*Vaccinium spp.*
Buttonbush	*Cephalanthus occidentalis*
Chinquapin	*Castanopsis spp.*
Chokeberry, red	*Aronia arbutifolia*
Chokecherry	*Prunus pennsylvanicas*
Common elderberry	*Sambucus canadensis*
Common spicebush	*Lindera benzoin*
Common witch hazel	*Hamamelis virginiana*
Currant	*Ribes spp.*
Dewberry	*Rebus spp.*
Dogwood	*Cornus spp.*
Dwarf huckleberry	*Gaylossacia dumosa*
Dwarf sumac	*Rhus copallina*
Early low blueberry	*Vaccinium vacillans*
Faragrant sumac	*Rhus aromatica*
Flowering dogwood	*Cornus florida*
Greenbrier (vine)	*Smilax spp.*
Gooseberry	*Ribes spp.*
Grape vine	*Vitis spp.*
Gray dogwood	*Cornus racemosa*
Hawthorne	*Crataegos spp.*
Hazelnut	*Corylus spp.*
Honeysuckle, red amur	*Lonicera maacki*
Honeysuckle, tatarian	*Lonicera tatarica*
Huckleberry	*Gaylussacia spp.*
Hydrangea, wild	*Hydrangea aborescens*
Ironwood	*Ostrya virginiana*
Japanese honeysuckle (vine)	*Lonicera japonica*
Juniper	*Juniperus spp.*
Nannyberry	*Viburnum lentago*

Common name	Scientific name
Northern honeysuckle	*Diervilla lonicera*
Partridgeberry (vine)	*Mitchella repens*
Pawpaw	*Asimina triloba*
Persimmon	*Diospyros virginiana*
Plum, wild	*Prunus americana*
Poison ivy (vine)	*Rhus radicans*
Redbud	*Cercis canadensis*
Red cedar	*Juniperus virginiana*
Red osier, dogwood	*Cornus stolonifera*
Rose	*Rosa spp.*
Rough leaf dogwood	*Cornus drummondi*
Russian olive	*Elaeagnus angustifolia*
Sand cherry	*Prunus depressa*
Sassafrass	*Sassafras albidum*
Serviceberry	*Amalanchier spp.*
Smooth sumac	*Rhus glabra*
Spaicebush	*Lindera benzoin*
Spirea	*Spirea spp.*
Staghorn sumac	*Rhus typhina*
Viburnum	*Viburnum spp.*
Virginia creeper	*Parthenocissus spp.*
Weigela	*Weigela spp.*
Wild crab	*Pyrys coronaria*
Willow	*Salix spp.*
Wintergreen (trailing vine)	*Gaultheria procumbens*

GRASSES

Common name	Scientific name
Barnyard grass	*Echinochloa crusgalli*
Big bluestem	*Poa ampla*
Bluebunch wheatgrass	*Agropyron spicatum*
Brome grass	*Bromus japonicus*
Canary grass	*Phalaris spp.*
Cheat grass (cheat)	*Baromus tectorum*
Columbia needle grass	*Stipa columbiana*
Crab grass	*Digitaria sanquinalis*
Cusick bluegrass	*Poa cusickii*
Foxtail grass	*Setaria glauca*
Green neddlegrass	*Stipa viridula*
Idaho fescue	*Festuca idahoensis*
Indiangrass	*Sorghastrum nutans*

Common name	Scientific name
Indian ricegrass	*Oryzopsis hymenoides*
Intermediate wheatgrass	*Agropyron intermedium*
Johnson grass	*Sorghstrum halpense*
June grass	*Koeleria cristata*
Kentucky bluegrass	*Poa pratensis*
Little bluestem	*Andropogan scoparius*
Manna grass	*Glyceria striata*
Mutton grass	*Poa fendleriana*
Reed	*Phragmites australis*
Orchardgrass	*Dactylis glomerata*
Smooth Bromegrass	*Bromus inermis*
Switchgrass	*Panicum virgatum*
Tall wheatgrass	*Agropyron elongatum*
Thickspike wheat grass	*Agropyron dasystachyum*
Timothy	*Phleum pratense*

FORBS

Common name	Scientific name
Arrowhead	*Sagittaria spp.*
Aster	*Aster azureus*
Beggarticks	*Biddens spp.*
Black-eyed susan	*Rudbeckia hirta*
Boneset	*Eupatorium perfoliatum*
Burdock	*Arctium minus*
Canadian thistle	*Cirsium arvense*
Cardinal flower	*Lobelia cardinalis*
Cattail	*Typha spp.*
Chicory	*Cichorium intybus*
Cinquefoil	*Potentilla simplex*
Cocklebur	*Xanthium strumarium*
Common fleabane	*Erigeron philadelphicus*
Common sunflower	*Helianthus annus*
Coneflower	*Rudbeckia fulgida*
Coyote tobacco	*Nicotiana attenuata*
Daisy fleabane	*Erigeron annuus*
Goldenrod	*Solidago spp.*
Hairy fleabane	*Erigeron concinnus*
Hawkweed	*Hieracium venosum*
Hoary phlox	*Phlox canescebs*
Horseweed	*Erigeron annuus*
Ironweed	*Vernonia altissima*

Common name	Scientific name
Joe-pye weed	*Eupatorium spp.*
Lambsquarter	*Chenopodium album*
Marsh marigold	*Caltha palustris*
Milkweed	*Asclepias syriaca*
Mint	*Mentha arvensis*
Ox-eye	*Heliopsis helianthoides*
Phlox	*Phlox dicaricata*
Plantain	*Plantago major*
Pondweed	*Potamogeton spp.*
Prickley pear	*Opuntia spp.*
Ragweed	*Ambrosia artemisiifolia*
Swamp milkweed	*Asclepias incarnata*
Skunk cabbage	*Symplocarpus foetidus*
Small white aster	*Aster vimineus*
Smartweed	*Polygonum spp.*
Teasel	*Dipsacus sylvestris*
Water plantain	*Alisma subcordatum*
Wild lettuce	*Lactuca canadensis*
Wild onion	*Allium stellatum*
Wild strawberry	*Fragaria virginiana*
Yarrow	*Achillea millefolium*

LEGUMES

Alfalfa	*Medicago sativa*
Sweet clover	*Melilotus officianalis*
Red clover	*Trifolium pratense*

FLOWERS

Bergamot	*Monarda didyma*
Bull thistle	*Cirsium vulgare*
Butterfly weed	*Asclepias tuberosa*
Canada thistle	*Cirsium arvense*
Cardinal flower	*Lobelia cardinalis*
Catchfly	*Silene spp.*
Catnip	*Nepeta cataria*
Columbines	*Aquilegia spp.*
Coralbells	*Heuchera sanguinea*
Dandelion	*Taraxacum officinale*
Four o'clocks	*Mirabilis spp.*

Common name	Scientific name
Marigold	*Tagetes spp.*
Mexican sunflower	*Tithonia sp.*
New England aster	*Aster novae-angliae*
Oxeye daisy	*Chrysanthemum sp.*
Pasture rose	*Rosa carolina*
Purple coneflower	*Echinacea purpurea*
Primrose	*Primula spp.*
Queen Anne's lace	*Daucus carota*
Rose of Sharon	*Hibiscus syriacus*
Trumpet creeper	*Campsis radicans*
Sage	*Salvia spp.*
Scarlet runner bean	*Phaseolus coccineus*
Spider flower	*Cleome sp.*
Zinnia	*Zinnia elegans*